A Celebrant's Guide

The Five Elements

Written by Veronika Sophia Robinson
Cover illustration by Sarah Esau

Published by
The Celebrant Collection,
An imprint of Starflower Press

The Five Elements
© Written by Veronika Sophia Robinson
© Cover art illustrated by Sarah Esau
978-1-7385324-1-4
Published by The Celebrant Collection,
Starflower Press
www.starflowerpress.com
Full Moon in Virgo, February 2024

Contents

"Remember that you are WATER
Cry. Cleanse. Flow. Let go.

Remember that you are FIRE
Burn. Tame. Adapt. Ignite.

Remember that you are AIR
Observe. Breathe. Focus. Decide.

Remember that you are EARTH
Ground. Build. Produce. Give.

Remember that you are SPIRIT
Connect. Listen. Know. Be still."
— Author Unknown

Dedicated to

She Who Creates

And my mother. Always my mother.
A naturally gifted ceremonialist:
rooted in rituals,
maker of magic,
wise woman,
weaver of words,
speaker of spells,
astute astrologer,
and Goddess of the Elements.

Ceremonial Work

Creating ceremonies with the five elements adds depth, richness, vibrancy and awareness of our place in the world. To do so, we need to consciously live and breathe them in our daily lives so that our understanding and experience of them fits like a second skin. As with any aspect of celebrant work, if we don't engage with something authentically it shows.

This book is intended for those either new to ritual-infused celebrancy or new to the idea of bringing the elemental energies into their craft. As you turn these pages, you'll be invited to reflect upon each element, and to befriend its qualities, capacities, symbols and vibrational correspondences. The more you engage with these, the richer your exploration will be and the more confidently you can bring the elements into your celebrant practice.

My experience of the elemental energies has been lifelong, and it is my joy to share with you some personal stories. By doing so, it is hoped that it will awaken your own memories. Although the elements are the basis of life, to actively engage with them in a ceremonialist capacity might trigger what is known as a 'witch wound'. For many of us (regardless of gender), there exists, at a cellular level, either ancestral or (if you believe/understand it as such) past-life memories.

A witch, despite culture's portrayal of her as an old woman in a pointy black hat with a wart-encrusted nose, caustic cackle, and hell-bent on causing harm, is a person *deeply connected to nature, the divine feminine,* and the *Cosmos.* Within her village, she'd be known as the medicine woman for her specialist knowledge and skills of plants, nature and energy. With each passing generation, this would be passed down the family line.

The memories of The Burning Times, for some people, is never far from the surface. During this darkened era of humanity, if you were a herbalist, healer, outspoken, independent, a midwife or diviner, your life was in danger. Historians believe around 50,000 innocent people were executed; some scholars, however, suggest it was 100,000 or more. The figure doubles for those who were exiled, tortured or imprisoned. The Witch Wound is often felt by those in modern times who are practitioners of energy awareness, earth-based medicines, rituals and ceremonies. It is believed that during the Little Ice Age, the drop in weather temperature led to famines, and repeated crop failures. People struggled to survive severe storms and chilly Winters. Rather than recognising it as an act of God/Nature, witches were often blamed for the impact this had on people's personal fortunes.

One of the ways this wound can be seen in modern times is a wariness of being visible in our work, and feeling uncomfortable talking about or sharing our passion for plants, herbs, nature and the elements.

My hope is that you'll own the gifts of your work and gently and fully express yourself, personally and professionally, with the elements as allies. As I explore them throughout this book, I shall do so in the order they appear in the zodiac: fire, earth, air, water.

Fire glows
Earth grows
Air blows
Water flows
And Spirit knows

- Author Unknown

At The Feet of My Mother

My whole childhood was an apprenticeship for becoming a Heart-led Celebrant. I didn't know it at the time, of course. As I look back across those early years, I can see so clearly how deeply ritual, the five elements, and reverence for life was embedded into my being.

Raised at the feet of an amazing astrologer, I learned about the nature of the elements not only physically but metaphysically and psychologically. As an adult, I became a second-generation astrologer. My younger daughter is the third generation of astrologers in the maternal line.

In these pages I shall share what I learned from my mother, and from my celebrant practice and work as a psychological astrologer. This is an exploration of the five elements (most people talk of four elements). I also include the fifth element in my life, personally and professionally. The reasons will become clear shortly.

You'll learn the qualities and energies of each element, and also how they interact with each other: whether it's in a challenging way or harmoniously.

By understanding this, and their vibrational connections and correspondences (both animate and inanimate), that are associated with them, you'll be able to integrate them into your practice with confidence.

What follows is my journey with the elements and some of the ways I've experienced them in my life. I share them in the hope it will allow your own memories to surface giving you the opportunity to reflect on the way the elements weave into your life.

My Fire

The day I arrived Earthside in Brisbane, Australia, it was a blistering hot Summer's day tucked midway between Christmas and New Year. From the moment I was born, this element made itself felt.

My earliest memory of the power of fire was when I was about five years old. For the duration of my childhood, my father worked in Papua New Guinea, an island country in the southwestern Pacific Ocean. As a Party

Exploration Manager, in charge of 2,000 men, he'd oversee mining operations in the tropical forests. One day, in order to rescue a family from their burning hut, my dad raced in there to move an oil drum before it caught fire. When my father returned home to us (in Australia), I was not allowed to see him for several weeks because the third-degree burns were so severe. Despite not seeing the fire myself, the impact of it on his life shaped me by default. I understood, even at that young age, the power of a flame.

A year or so later, we left our suburban home at the edges of Brisbane and moved to a 700-acre property on the Darling Downs in south-east Queensland. It was here that I'd experience the power of fire once again. It hadn't taken long for me to fall in love with the landscape around me: fields, grassy hills and eucalyptus-clad mountains, and a creek with crystal-clear water flowing the length of our property. We had seventy horses. My childhood was lived on the back of a horse, and much of my time (when not in school) was spent riding up the mountains. I knew the land well. This place was my home, and I cherished the open spaces and immense freedom to roam and explore.

Australia is a continent prone to ravaging wildfires. A combination of intense heat, wild winds fuelling the tiniest of flames, and volatile oils in the leaves of a eucalyptus, and the combustible nature of tinder-dry grasses, make it an inferno just waiting to happen.

When raging fires scorched our land, it caused devastation unlike anything I'd ever known in my young life. All that remained was a charcoaled-landscape, scorched tree trunks, and cremated carcasses of koalas, kangaroos, lizards and other animals. At the time, I was about ten years old. The event changed my life.

As I made my way through the burnt forest, my footsteps disturbing the fallen ash, I knew I wanted to be a writer. I needed to write. The loss around me begged to be expressed.

In my home state of Queensland, there is an old tradition of Burning Off. I've seen it used to burn off dead or dry scrubland under managed conditions. This technique is employed to prevent wildfires destroying large tracts of land. It was something my father did on our property. The fire, carefully managed, would sweep through all the dry grasses. After the next rain, beautiful, lush, green grass sprouted from the charred remains. New life. *Transformation.*

There was also the joy of building a bonfire. After any storm, we'd gather fallen branches and add them to a pile until it was big enough to burn. This was another way of minimising the amount of dead and dry wood in the tree-filled areas, potentially lessening the impact of a wildfire.

When I left home, in my mid-teens, I moved to the Adelaide Hills in South Australia. During these years, I rented the loveliest flat: a pine-wood mezzanine space on the same property as the Peace Research Institute. My home, with floor-to-ceiling windows, overlooked an elm forest. Workshops and events were often held at the institute. When I heard about a firewalking workshop, I signed up. I was just 19. We spent the afternoon building the fire up until the flames went out and what remained were hot coals. Everyone took their turn to cross over the three-metre expanse. Fear inched its way through my entire body. That is, until the facilitator's five-year-old daughter danced across the coals. My internal voice went something like this: "I'm not going to be upstaged by a kid!" and off I walked across 600C coals like a pro. Not a single burn or blister! A couple of years later, I chose to go firewalking again. I realised that if I could overcome my fear and *belief* that I'd be burnt, and emerge unscathed, well, I could set my mind to anything. (The word firewalking is a misnomer as you're walking on coals rather than fire.)

The hearth of our rural home here in Cumbria is lit by beeswax candles and fairylights. Candlelight offers me the element of fire in a way that's comforting and nurturing. Although blessed by the reliable warmth of central heating, both living rooms feature a woodburning stove. There's a beauty to a real fire and the lifeforce that it brings to a home. Of course, it's there for warmth during a power outage or when the weather is below zero outside and the house could do with a boost, but it is also a welcome friend. I can sit for a long time just gazing into the flames without a need for conversation, music or other distraction. The flames feed my senses.

Around the firepit in the garden, I gather with friends and family to share in baking damper. We've been to the woods, gathered sticks and cleaned them up. While our 'stick bread' is held over the flames and coals, we tap into something primordial: fire. Each of us is content. Far removed from mobile phones and other screens, we're connected to the element and each other.

Today, as I edit these pages, it's minus 4C outside. As an Australian living in the far north of England, my bones yearn for days where the temperature is above 20C (30C and higher is heaven for me). Sunlight is one of my favourite things in this world, and to bask in hot sunshine is a pleasurable pastime.

My Earth

My first memory of the element of earth was when I was about four. At the time, we lived in a wooden house opposite scrubland (uncleared native bush in Australia). I was the youngest child, at that stage, and had two older brothers and an older sister. Naturally, I wanted to follow them everywhere. The last thing my brothers wanted was a pesky and curious little girl following them. And curious I was! They'd obviously decided enough was enough and made a plan. I watched them cross the road and head into the scrubland. Wearing my pretty little white frilly socks and new shoes, I secretly followed them along the path. I could see them in the distance and walked quietly. And then, all of a sudden, I fell into a hole. It wasn't big. Maybe about a foot deep. It was filled with runny mud! They'd covered it in dried grasses to camouflage it, and I'd dropped right into it. My beautiful white socks, now chocolate brown, were completely ruined. Their laughter was something I'll never forget.

While most little girls were playing with dolls, I lived in a world of dirt, dust and Matchbox cars. I couldn't have been happier! There, with dusty knees, I'd pave roads, build cities, and drive through these places. I even remember eating dirt (way beyond toddler age) just to fully experience it. Though I don't eat dirt anymore, I do love the scent of it when I'm on my knees gardening. I don't think I'm ever more alive than when I'm connected in this way; hands in the soil. Apart from when I have to go out to work or shopping, my life is generally spent barefoot. Throughout the year I regularly walk on the grass in the garden and ground myself. I also sleep with an 'earthing sheet'.

Amongst my favourite scents is petrichor: the earthy smell of rain when it meets dry soil.

For as long as I've had to cook, it's brought me pleasure. It activates my senses and engages me. From garden to plate, I'm connecting with the earth element.

My Air

The electrical storms of my motherland, Australia, are something to be experienced. When I was a young child, one of my favourite things to do was head outside and play beneath the growling thunder and flashes of lightning. To this day (even though storms here in Cumbria are timid in comparison), I come alive during a thunder storm. It exhilarates me.

"Let's go fly a kite!" sang Mary Poppins from the first record I ever owned. The day of my wedding, at Green Bay in Auckland, New Zealand, there was an incoming cyclone. Although we ended up having our ceremony indoors in a wee chapel, we headed out to the beach for photos and I flew a kite on my wedding day.

My relationship with this element fascinates me. On one hand, I have a phobia about not having enough fresh air to breathe, and need the window open every day of the year (my nose risks frostbite midwinter when I'm asleep). That first 'sip' of air, pre-dawn, when I walk in the garden is absolutely divine. Yet, I detest the wind. For some reason, it always feels like a battle. As a celebrant, I've lost count of how many ceremonies I've officiated in gale-force winds. I have, however learned to embrace the invisible energies of this element and when she shows her face in my ceremonies I welcome the wild winds in for she clearly has something to say and wants her presence felt. Quite recently I officiated a Handfasting Ceremony at the Callanish Stones on the Isle of Lewis in the Outer Hebrides, Scotland. My couple had travelled over from Australia. So much time and energy, from all of us, was placed in that ceremony. And then, Mrs Wind howled her way through every single moment. "Windiest altar known to man" my bride said to me the other day. I had no choice but to beckon the air in and adlib my way through the 'failed' candle lighting.

For most of my childhood, I dreamt I could fly. It was so easy! I'd be running down the grassy hill just behind our home and then take off into the air. I don't recall ever having a dream like that as an adult. I often dreamt of plane crashes, too, where I'd see them coming down; and then I'd head over to those who'd passed away and help their souls to 'rise'. Despite those dreams, to fly on a plane always excites me (not the cramped seat, snoring men, screaming babies bit); the take off and ascent is wonderful!

My sense of smell is acute, and so the air around me needs to be clean or pleasant: fresh air, essential oils, incense, the scent of wild apples, lilac, eucalyptus, roses and jasmine soothe me. My favourite scent memories include: the smell of my newborn daughters; walking with my mother through a Tasmanian eucalyptus forest after a storm; freesias growing in our sub-tropical courtyard; fresh-cut lemongrass from our garden; Mum massaging my back with Vicks Vapour Rub; petrichor; German Christmas baking: lebkuchen and stollen.

My Water
My earliest memory, and most certainly some of my favourite memories in this life, involve water.

At just three, we had a swimming pool in the back garden. It was circular, and overhead was a string of coloured lights. There was a foam floatie that I wore on my back when I went swimming. Except for the time I didn't! My mother recalled finding me in the pool looking up at her through the water. In our next home, we had a pool too. This was large, oval, and big enough for my brothers to paddle their dinghies in.

Nearby, was Dead Horse Creek. A hangout place for teenagers. I was only six, but I'd tag along with my sister Heidi. There were no dead horses, thankfully, but we sure had fun splashing and swinging from a vine into the water. And then, we moved a couple of hours away, to our 700-acre property. On this land, we learnt a lot about water. With seventy horses to water, a handful of children to raise, and trying to survive a seven-year drought, a rainwater tank supply was never going to do the job. My parents had three bore holes drilled. What a blessing to live above an artesian basin (underground lake) and have an unlimited water supply. Despite the dry landscape around us, my mum's four-acre garden became a Garden of Eden. She had those sprinklers spraying out water 24/7 and our lawns were vibrant green, and the trees flourished in that sub-tropical weather.

Along the base of our mountain flowed a creek. How can I ever forget the taste of that crystal-clear water, as I knelt down on the granite rock, with my hands cupped, as I brought that pure aqua to my lips? There was never a shortage of fun and adventure for us kids. A favourite activity during floods was to don a parka (jacket) underneath a raincoat and float down the creek for a couple of miles. We'd have to hike the long walk home but it was worth it for the adventure.

We often played in the creek too, though I'll never forget the time my sister Heidi and I cooked up a meal over a fire and she went to wash the pan in the creek. It slipped out of her hands and started disappearing with the current. Heidi caught the pan just as it was going over the waterfall!

At the bottom of the waterfall was a natural dam. As kids, we couldn't have been more blessed. Our home was an adventure playground. The thing about the dam was that none of us ever reached the bottom. Even in times of drought, when the creek became almost dry, we couldn't get to the base. One of our 'party tricks' was to invite our friends from the city over for the weekend and take them swimming in the dam. A dam with leeches! Of course, we knew what they were, and how to dispose of them, but it was pretty terrifying for our friends.

We had a couple of other dams too. These were manmade and muddy. In some ways, they were even more fun. My two favourite elements together: earth and water. What a sight we looked when we came home! No wonder my mother's washing machine was on seven days a week. Painting ourselves in mud was a fairly regular part of my childhood.

As a young adult living in South Australia, my adventures continued. I'd often go wild camping with friends. If we were down the peninsula, there'd be magical evenings watching seals and dolphins splash about in the moonlight.

During my pregnancy with my elder daughter, I swam with dolphins off the coast of New Zealand. When motherhood met me, I gave birth in water in the privacy of our bedroom. My research during pregnancy inspired me to set up the National Waterbirth Trust in New Zealand.

My last memory of wild swimming, as an adult, was definitely in a much warmer climate than I live in now. My thermoception (sense of *heat*) is such that the cold triggers nociception (my perception of *pain*). So many of my friends go wild swimming (even in water with ice at the edges!). I admire them but I'm a hot-water girl. I've soaked in secret hot springs in New Zealand and luxuriated in an outdoor hot tub on New Year's Eve in Pennsylvania as snow flakes fell around us. On that same holiday, my friend Amy and I enjoyed ice skating on a canal in New Jersey.

I've always been naturally at home in the water. As much as I thrive in this element, I've a certain fear for 'too much' water. When my old beau, John, would take me out sailing in his yacht off the coast in Hawke's Bay, New Zealand, I'd often get seasick even while wearing seasickness bands.

On one of my ferry sailings to Ireland, I was rather green as we travelled through a turbulent storm across wild waves.

Living in Cumbria, I quickly realised just how many rivers, becks and streams there are here. When floods arrive, you can quickly find yourself unable to get anywhere. More than that, though, I can't bear driving over bridges when rivers are in flood. My legs turn to jelly. I like my water 'contained'.

These are my happy places: jacuzzi, hot tub, thermal spring, steam room, heated pool.

Anyone who knows me well, will have noticed I always have water with me. I can't bear even a hint of dehydration.

The day I wrote this section, I'd spent an afternoon on a steamer sailing around Lake Ullswater with my favourite funeral director. The winds were high and the waters choppy. The mountains around us stood still and solid in the drizzly rain. Earth and Water.

My spirit animal is the sea turtle (symbolising the water and earth elements, both of which are strong in me and my life).

My Spirit

As far back as I can remember, I always had a sense there was something 'more'. If I had known what it was, I'd have been able to adequately answer my younger daughter,

Eliza, when she was three and asked: "What's at the end of forever!" According to science, the Universe is always expanding (and it's doing so at faster and faster speeds).

As a child, my desire to become a nun was so strong. I've no doubt it was a past life memory.

My need for ritual, connection with the divine, and living with reverence infused my days. I also wasn't averse to bargaining with God, either. My mother had built me the most beautiful house (like a Wendy House). A short walk from our home, through bushes, was an old dunny (outdoor toilet). Mum transformed it into a shop for me: verandah, windows, lino, curtains. It was brilliant! The joy of having such a creative mother is that it enhanced my childhood in many ways. However, to get to my gorgeous shop I had to walk through an area that was likely to have snakes. Snakes are my number one fear. Not death. Not public speaking. Not heights. Not starvation. Not dying in a fire. Snakes! So, every time I trekked up to that shop, God and I had this conversation. Well, actually, it was a monologue. It went something like this: "If you're really there God, don't let me see any snakes. If you LOVE me, God, don't let me see any snakes!" I never heard God answer me in words. I never saw any snakes, either.

The fifth element is Spirit. If you're atheist or humanist, feel free to simply think of this element as sky (although the sky ends about 62 miles from Earth, and that is the start of outer space).

As a child, on our kitchen wall we had a large poster of The Desiderata by Max Ehrmann.

"You are a child of the Universe, no less than the trees and the stars; you have a right to be here." Every time I sat down to eat, I read those life-enhancing words. Can you imagine the power of that as a daily affirmation? You could say I lived beneath the stars (well, we all do). My mother and I often slept outside all night. We'd set up camp on the trampoline (off the ground away from snakes; have I mentioned my fear of snakes?), snuggled beneath our duvets and with comfy pillows. And there, beneath the great, open unpolluted night skies were the Southern Hemisphere constellations. These are permanently etched into my mind and heart. Even now, after living more than half my life outside of Australia, and two and a half decades in the Northern Hemisphere,

I still don't know the skies here in England. In one sense, it's hard to go to sleep when you're beneath the majesty of something as magnificent as the night sky. It draws you. You wait for a falling star. You imagine life elsewhere. All at once you feel connected to everything (child of the Universe, no less than the stars) and at another level feel utterly insignificant. More than forty-five years later, in a much colder clime, I like to step outside pre-dawn, and just before I go to bed at night, and connect with the night sky. It reminds me of my place in this world. I am at one with everything.

I often yearn to take my comfy mattress outside at night just to lay beneath the stars again. Instead, I watch them through my bedroom window and connect to something light years away, and yet also within me.

Silence and stillness, to me, belong to the element of Spirit.

Elemental Journey

Before you read any further, take some time to reflect on your own experiences with the elements.

Fire

What is your first memory of fire?

Has fire been a theme at different times of your life?

What are your pleasant memories of fire?

Do you have any unpleasant memories or experiences of fire?

Earth

What is your first memory of earth?

Has earth been a theme at different times of your life?

What are your pleasant memories of earth?

Do you have any unpleasant memories or experiences of earth?

Air

What is your first memory of air?

Has air been a theme at different times of your life?

What are your pleasant memories of air?

Do you have any unpleasant memories or experiences of this element?

Water

What is your first memory of water?

Has water been a theme at different times of your life?

What are your pleasant memories of water?

Do you have any unpleasant memories or experiences of water?

Spirit

What is your first memory of Spirit?

Has Spirit been a theme at different times of your life?

What are your pleasant memories of Spirit?

Do you have any unpleasant memories or experiences of Spirit?

Elementally:

Fire is dry and hot,
Earth is dry and cold.
Air is wet and hot,
Water is wet and cold

Our Primordial Roots

When we take a shamanic or holistic approach to working and living with the five elements, we tap into ancient roots and thread this connection to the divine within all beings. We are, at once, specialists in ritual who perform healing rites in our communities as artists, magicians and storytellers. That is, we are *celebrants*. When we recognise the altar of Mother Earth, and bow with reverence to all her offerings, our ceremonial rites of passage are elevated.

In this book you'll learn the vibrational connections and correspondences which resonate with each element, and how they're symbolised in nature or manmade ways. You'll see ways to weave them in rituals and ceremonies as choreography and narrative. You'll also have suggestions about how to bring it into more focus in your personal life. You'll understand how to tap into elemental vocabulary to infuse your narrative. There is guidance about elemental energy exchanges as well as the four basic human personalities based on four elements.

May you be inspired by this practical exploration of the five elements, and may it infuse your work with a richness and quality that goes on to touch many lives, including your own.

"Don't dismiss the elements.
Water soothes and heals.
Air refreshes and revives.
Earth grounds and holds.
Fire is a burning reminder of our own will
and creative power.
Swallow their spells.
There's a certain sweet comfort
in knowing that you belong to them all."
— **Victoria Erickson**

Elemental Vibrational Matches

Directions

Fire - South
Earth - North
Air - East
Water - West
Spirit - As Above, So below; Everywhere

Time

Fire - Noon
Earth - Midnight
Air - Sunrise
Water - Sunset
Spirit - Eternal and infinite

Seasons

Fire - Summer
Earth - Winter
Air - Springtime
Water - Autumn
Spirit - Recurring Seasons

Gender

Fire - Masculine
Earth - Feminine
Air - Masculine
Water - Feminine
Spirit – No Gender/All Genders

Zodiac Signs

Fire - Aries, Leo, Sagittarius
Earth - Taurus, Virgo, Capricorn
Air - Gemini, Libra, Aquarius
Water - Cancer, Scorpio, Pisces
Spirit - Circle in the centre of the birth chart; all signs; trascendence of signs

Colours

Fire - Red, gold, yellow, crimson, orange
Earth - Green, brown, black
Air - Blue, white, yellow
Water - Blue, green, turquoise, aquamarine, silver, grey
Spirit - White, purple, silver, black

Ritual Tools

Fire - Athame (knife), sword
Earth - Pentacle, coins, salt, soil
Air - Wand, feather
Water - Cup, bowl, chalice, cauldron
Spirit - Spiral, light, infinity symbol, helix

Instruments

Fire – Trumpets, trombones, tubas, French horns, drumming (with sticks)
Earth – Singing, percussion, saxophone, double bass, hand-on animal-hide drum (shamanic)
Air – Flute, clarinet, tin whistle
Water – Harp, cello, classical guitar
Spirit – Self-contained

Botanicals

Fire: Rosemary, sunflower and palm, marigold, amaranth, snapdragon, calendula, sagebrush, stinging nettle, holly, cedar, mace, thistle

Earth: Ivy, nuts, cypress, oak, moss, fern bark, acorns

Air: Lemongrass, pine, violets, dill, aspen, bergamot, marjoram, vervain, poppy, dandelion, dandelion seeds, chamomile, yarrow, dill, fennel, poplar, frankincense, peppermint

Water: Succulents, lily, seaweed, lemon balm, aloe, lotus, willow, kelp, cucumber, lilac, pear

Spirit: Lotus, apple, chestnut, ash

Gems, Crystals and Stones

Fire – Red jasper, amber, carnelian, ruby, garnet, bloodstone

Earth – Emerald, jade, tourmaline, onyx, quartz, amethyst, granite, amber, moss agate, Tiger's eye

Air – Sapphire, topaz, smoky quartz, clear quartz, pumice, amber*, blue kyanite

Water – Blue tourmaline, aquamarine, opal, blue topaz, coral, pearl

Spirit – Amethyst, pearl, quartz, opal
amber may be used for fire, earth and air.

Foods

Fire – Jalapeños, juniper, cumin, cloves, saffron, coriander, cacti, marigold, cinnamon, mustard, chilli, ginger, allspice, red pepper, poppy seeds, curry, marmalade, oranges

Earth – Sweet potato, beetroot, onion, garlic, cashews, dates, pickles, bread, nuts, grains

Air – Chickweed, lentils, popcorn, tofu, puffed rice

Water – Watermelon, coconut, strawberries, apple

Spirit – Honey, mead

Animals

Fire - Tiger, lion, wasp, scorpion, shark, horse

Earth - Bear, worm, cow, wolf, stag, creatures which burrow, bull, hare

Air - Wren, eagle, blackbird, hawk, raven, bee, dragonfly, butterfly, bats

Water - Dolphin, whale, turtle, seal, otter, frog, fish, starfish, barnacle, swan, crane, geese

Spirit - Dove

Elemental Spirits

Fire - Djinn, dragon, chimera, phoenix, salamander

Earth - Dwarves, gnomes, trolls, fairies, dryads

Air - Zephyrs, sylphs, winged fairies and sprites.

Water - Kelpie, Nymph, Undine, Cailleach, water fairies

Spirit - World Tree, Sphinx

Fire

"Carry your heart through this world like a life-giving Sun."
— Hafiz

In my home, the hearth fire is a feature in our main living area. Although used for warmth, the residents who once lived in our 18th Century Cumbrian cottage would have considered this the heart of the home: the kitchen. Over the flames they'd have stirred a large pot with their simmering stews. In the Wintertime, I simmer mulled grape juice in the same place as those who lived here hundreds of years ago.

Whether we light the fire in our hearth, stand beneath the warmth of the Sun, or call on the fire-god Agni, this element reminds us that the Sun is essential for light and warmth and creation.

The most obvious representation of fire in our lives is the Sun. Close your eyes and think about how the Sun's rays gently warm your skin. Without fire, we wouldn't be able to cook food, warm ourselves, or have light when the Sun has set. Our ancestors relied on fire to scare off predators.
The element of fire has been revered in ritual for over five thousand years. As ceremonialists, we have called upon the sacred flame as well as honoured the inner flame of our heart centre.

Fire *creates*. Fire *destroys*.

From amidst the ashes, new life grows after a wildfire.

Energetically, we use the element of fire to open our heart, to burn negativity, to fulfil desires.

As an element, we look at themes of creativity, illumination, transformation, passion, strength, brightness, charisma, vitality, and movement. Fire is the only element we can't touch without being harmed.

To exist, fire needs to consume another element. Despite its power, it can also be extinguished by water, earth and air. There's no ignoring fire. It's captivating and mesmerising.

The energy of the fire element is seen in:

- Sun
- Sunlight
- Deserts
- Volcanoes
- Summer

Fire
Burn
Tame
Adapt
Ignite

"In each moment the fire rages,
it will burn away a hundred veils.
And carry you a thousand steps
toward your goal."
— Rumi

Fire in Ceremonial Work

"Don't fear the light within.
May it ignite the Sacred Flame in your soul."
— Paulo Coelho

Fire, as an element and primordial energy, is revered in cultures and religions around the world. Considered the sacred flame, it is recognised for its power to move quickly and spread wildly.

Candles
Candles can be used in different ways: to symbolise a person's quality or a desired intention, for example. It might have further symbolism depending on its colour, scent or what wax has been used.

Sunflowers
Sunflowers not only remind us of the Sun, they also tilt their heads towards the Sun throughout the day. They symbolise the element of fire, and are used to denote joy, luck and enthusiasm.

Amber
Amber has been referred to as 'Tears of the Sun'. We use it in rituals to symbolise courage and

protection. Even though amber is the fossilised sap from a tree and may be considered as corresponding to earth, some elementalists use it under fire because of its colour, and others under air because of the bubbles it contains.

Charcoal
Charcoal can be used in many ways, such as banishing negative energy, purifying space, and cleansing. It could be used to write something in a ritual, or ground up and sprinkled in the ceremonial space.

Lantern
Lanterns are a wonderful tool in ceremonial work. Consider them a symbol of illumination.

Solar Water
When I was a child, my mother didn't take us to doctors. Our ailments and illnesses were treated holistically. One of those ways was with solar water. To do this, she'd place a glass or glass jug out in the sunlight all day. It would be wrapped in coloured cellophane, and the rays of sunlight would shine through the colour and infuse the water with its energy. For example, 'blue' water eased headaches. 'Red' water gave my shy brother some extra confidence.

Use it in healing ceremonies (either imbibed or as a libation, or sprinkling).

Wood Ash
The ash from wood works well in any ritual where you want to symbolise change and rebirth.

Mango Nectar
The nectar of this tropical fruit works beautifully in anointing rituals for naming ceremonies. It symbolises happiness, love and friendship.

Ruby
Ruby is used in rituals as a symbol of courage, energy and passion.

Athame (knife)
Use this in a ceremony to symbolise the fire element, and cast a circle or open a circle.

Gold
Bring gold into a ceremony to remind us of the Sun. This high-vibrational colour can be used in ritual to symbolise power.

Spices
Use cayenne pepper, to spark up a relationship

Chilli to burn away negativity
Call on cloves for love and clarity.

Marigold
This bright flower is connected with the Sun. Although we would therefore match it to the fire energies of warmth, creativity and passion, traditionally, in the language of flowers, it meant *pain* and *grief*. It is used during the Mexican festival, *Day of the Dead*, to aid spirits in finding their way home. Be mindful of reflecting the culture of your client. For example, in Hinduism marigolds symbolise brightness. In Romania, sunlight and healing. Buddhists offer them as a symbol of respect and admiration.

Garnet
Dark red garnet serves not only in rituals for protection but also when we want to imbue the person with energy and passion. Great for a career-change ceremony.

Carnelian
This gem symbolises the Sun, and comes in orange or deep red. Consider using this in ceremonies where you want to draw on the energies of power, strength and courage.

Fire is the only element
we can't touch
without being harmed.

Examples of Fire-Element Rituals

Ritual: *Releasing Old Flames*
Fire is a primordial element of transformation. We'll draw on this power now to release words, actions and connections to old flames so that you can move freely into your marriage with each other. The words you wrote about these relationships are each in a bowl here, for your eyes only. Please read through what you've written, and if you still feel inclined to release them, then say them in your mind or out loud, if you like, and place them into the fire.
(Tammy and Dave release their connection to former relationships into the burning bowl)

Funerary Ritual: *Candle Lighting*
This candle will be lit by Suzi to symbolise the light Rani brought to this world.
(Suzi to light candle)
(And then, at the end of the ceremony)
Ritual: *Blowing out of the Candle*
For the last little while, we have lived in the light of our memories of Rani. We acknowledge that her story is over now, and to symbolise this we blow out the candle. Harriet, will you do this for us please?
(Harriet to blow out the candle)

Funerary Ritual: *Home-brewed Nettle Beer*
Today we've heard many stories about Brayden's adventures. Stories to sustain us during grief, and to accompany us well into the future. Brayden's life is an inspiring example of what it means to live life fully.

As the next piece of music plays, you're invited to enjoy a glass of Brayden's home-brewed nettle beer. Take a moment, while you sip, to imagine him out in these fields gathering bags of nettles in the Springtime to create his concoction.

The ancients would throw bundles of nettles onto the fire as an offering to the God of Thunder, Thor, for protection. Nettles are also associated with the threshold between life and death.
(*As the music plays, pass out beer to each mourner who would like some*)

Funerary Ritual: *Sunflower Coffin Blessing*
Katy-Lyn, we remember your love of the colour yellow, and give you this sunflower as a symbol that you are loved dearly and deeply, and of our gratitude for who you were and how you will remain in our hearts.

(touch the coffin three times with the sunflower, before placing it down)

Funerary Ritual: *Amber Amulet*
Before we lay Petani to rest, her grandmother, Moana, will wrap this amber amulet around her tiny wrist. (*Moana wraps the amulet*)

Petani, may you always be protected.
May you walk through the heavens with angels by your side. May you know that you were loved and you are loved.

Wedding Ritual: *Candle Lighting*
The lighting of candles in ceremony is as old as mankind. We instinctively call upon the power of fire - the lighting of the ways - and its capacity to illuminate our journey.

Today, we shall formally open this ceremony with the lighting of six candles as we bless the way forward for Tobias and Clara.

We shall call upon six guiding people in their lives; people who have loved, influenced, shaped and encouraged them. Let us begin with the maternal influence, for wise and nurturing feminine energies are at the heart of every sacred ceremony.

Ann, as Clara's mother, the woman who brought her into this world, would you please light the first candle?
(lights candle)
This candle you have lit is for courage and kindness, for these are qualities that Clara admires about you.

We reverently ask that kindness be a guiding light in this marriage.

Enid, as Tobias's mother, will you please light the second candle?
(lights candle)
Tobias honours your role as the matriarch, and that you have always stood so gracefully as the guiding light in his family. We ask this light now to continue to shine brightly in their marriage.

Sylvia, your role in Clara's life has not gone unnoticed. As her step-mother, would you do us all the honour of lighting the third candle?
(lights candle)
Sylvia, your innate maternal and loving qualities are being drawn upon today, for you have been a strong and positive influence in Clara's life. May your gifts go forward with her this day.

And now we draw upon the strength and solidity of the masculine energies within both families today.

Mikel, as Clara's father, will you please light our fourth candle?
(lights candle)
We honour you today for being such an inspirational and endlessly generous influence in this couple's life. May your spirit shine upon them this day and across the years ahead.

Our fifth candle in today's Lighting of the Ways ritual, will be lit by Tobias's father, Jonny.
(lights candle)
In every ancestral line, one would hope to find someone who models the essence of such a fine gentleman as yourself. Tobias considers you to embody the archetype of the wise owl, and so this day we ask that your wisdom weave its way through the days and nights as they write upon the pages of their unfolding story.

Hamish, you became part of Clara's family when you married Ann. Today, you are invited to light our final candle.
(lights candle)
This candle is for your ability to be unwaveringly supportive, a quality that has

proved to be a firm foundation. It is hoped that your lighting of the candle will symbolise the support of everyone here today.

Thank you to each of you for lighting the way.

Wedding ritual: *Sunflower Circle*
This day has been imbued with the brightness and beauty of sunflowers. They naturally enhance any space. As humans, we gravitate to the sunny and positive cheer of a sunflower. These flowers teach us to:
Stretch towards the light,
Hold ourselves high,
And cast out seeds of joy.

A sunflower circle will be created for Linnie and Gemma to stand in during their ceremony. The flowers symbolise longevity, love and loyalty; and the seeds remind us of new beginnings.

Bessie, as Linnie's mother, would you please place one of these sunflowers here?
(*Bessie places sunflower*)
Bessie, it is your ability to be decisive and determined which has shown Linnie and Gemma that you're passionate and have a strong sense of who you are. They wish to take this into their married life with them.

Judith, as Gemma's mother, would you please place a sunflower over here?
(*Judith places sunflower*)
Judith, you were born with a gift for always seeing the best in people. It is a quality that Gemma and Linnie hope to take forward with them.

Alice, as Linnie's sister, would you please place a sunflower into the circle?
(*Alice places sunflower*)
Alice, you have a natural ability to make beautiful things and are gifted at baking. It is hoped that this affinity with beauty will imbue their lives.

Hailey, would you please place a sunflower here? (*Hailey places sunflower*)
Hailey, you just light up any room! Linnie and Gemma would love nothing more than to infuse their days with the joy, humour and zest for life that you so readily share with others.

Max, would you please place a sunflower?
(*Max places sunflower*)
Max, it is your thoughtfulness and resilience that have inspired Linnie and Gemma, and so we ask that these traits accompany them on their passage as a married couple.

Billy, would you please place a sunflower?
(*Billy places sunflower*)
Billy, you walk through this world from such a place of love. Linnie and Gemma trust that they can take all they've learned from you, and bring that to their marriage.

Cindy, would you please place a sunflower?
(*Cindy places sunflower*)
Cindy, today we call upon your innate qualities of kindness, generosity and consideration, and ask that these be guiding values in Linnie and Gemma's married life.

Adam, you have two jobs! Firstly, could you please place the final sunflower?
(*Adam places sunflower*)
Adam, you have such a loving heart. Every day this inspires Linnie and Gemma. Our wish today is that they can bring that beautiful loving essence into their relationship.

Will you scatter these sunflowers seeds around the circle, in between the flowers?
(*scatters sunflower seeds*)
Adam, these are the seeds of kindness. And just as you are kind, may Linnie and Gemma bring kindness to each other, and all those people who happen upon their path.

(circle is cast)

Linnie and Gemma, this is your sacred space where you'll make your vows, pledges and promises.

Wedding Ritual: *Charcoal Challenge*

Historically, charcoal was used for writing. Did you know there are charcoal-etched cave drawings that are 28,000 years old? Today Lindsey and Scott are using charcoal to express their creativity. Charcoal is a symbol of transformation. Marriage is quite the rite of passage if you're looking to be transformed!

Even though they're both such talented professional artists neither of them has ever drawn each other and nor have they ever worked with charcoal before. This challenge will show them, and us, just how well they'll meet the challenges of life. They will sit with their backs to you so that you can see how their drawing is going, but they won't be able to see each other's portrait until they've finished.

(their favourite song plays while they're sketching)

Wedding Ritual: *The Spice of Marriage*
(Have several bowls and pouring vessels on the table to scoop or pour)

Leigh and Lenny are foodies and adore cooking. Food doesn't just provide nutrients, it's also a source of pleasure as is the art of cooking. This ritual honours the Spice of Marriage.

Leigh and Lenny, as you come into marriage, you're combining your individual talents, skills and gifts. Your personalities merge. The union of marriage is a mix of: who we are, and who we are when we're with the one we love.

Just as your gifts combine, so too do spices combine to complete a recipe. You've each said that you complete each other. The spices that you'll blend in a moment will integrate and never be the same again. By choosing to marry, we acknowledge that your lives will never be the same again. You'll begin by each pouring salt. Once you both add salt to this bowl, the individual grains will never be separated. Salt has long been recognised for its properties of preservation. It is a symbol of protection. Our wish is that your marriage will always be protected.
(Lenny and Leigh to pour salt)

Ginger is the spice of passion, and also attracts wealth. May your marriage be abundant with all the blessings of life. Lenny please add the ginger.
(Lenny to add the ginger)

Cinnamon is the spice of stability and warmth. May your love, home and days be blessed with comforts and pleasure. To this mix, Leigh will you please add cinnamon?
(adds cinnamon)

Listening and togetherness are essential in a happy marriage. To symbolise this, we draw on the spice cumin. Lenny will you please add this?
(pours cumin)

Adventure has been the cornerstone of your relationship, leading you to beautiful places around the world. Today we draw on black, green and white pepper. These symbolise wealth and adventure, something we hope continues throughout all the days of your married life. Leigh, could you please add the pepper?
(adds pepper)
Sage is the herb of wisdom and long life. May each of you always have the wisdom to come

from a place of kindness and care, both in word and deed. Lenny, will you please add the sage?
(add the sage)

Who knows the twists and turns that your lives will take? We draw on the symbolism of turmeric today for it speaks of adaptability. Leigh, can you please add the turmeric?
(adds turmeric)

Just as turmeric can remind us to adapt, mustard symbolises how we deal with challenges. May you both rise to the challenges of life, understanding that there are always choices. Lenny, could you please add the mustard?
(adds mustard)

The last addition to the mix is rosemary. This symbolises love and remembrance.
Leigh, would you please add the rosemary?
(adds rosemary)

Leigh and Lenny, would you please both add more salt to the mix?
(pour salt)

(To the guests) In cultures around the world, no matter where people live, eating a meal

together is a wedding tradition. Leigh and Lenny will be sharing food today with you: the important people in their lives. Gather round now as they cook your choice of chicken or tofu using their wedding spice!
(*bite-sized pieces are coated in spice and then cooked on the BBQ*)

Funeral Favour: *Scattering Seeds of Kindness*
There are some people who are impossible to forget. Gladys was one of those people. We'll remember her in so many ways and how she lit up our lives like sunshine. In a few moments, you're invited to take a handful of these Lesser Celandine seeds. You can plant them here, today, in this woodland, or place them in one of these bags and take them away. Plant them in memory of Gladys. In your garden. In this woodland. On open ground.

Scatter those seeds in the same way that Gladys scattered seeds of kindness wherever she went. Long before the other woodland flowers bloom, these beautiful flowers peep up to gladden our hearts with their lovely bright faces. In ancient times, the Celts called them 'grian' which means 'Sun'. Today we remember the arc of shining light that was Gladys's life from her sunrise on April 1st 1933 to the setting Sun on December 27th 2019.

(Each mourner is welcome to gather a handful of seeds and follow me into the woodland to scatter them far and wide)

Funerary Ritual: *Red Marbles*

Watching the person we have loved our whole lives become riddled with aggressive dementia steals something from them and us. Jackson, in his more lucid moments, would become distraught as he expressed that he was 'losing his marbles'. Even though he's now free from this debilitating illness, the residual effect on the family will last the rest of their lives. Each of Jackson's five children will pick up a red marble from this bowl. As they do so, they will share a memory they have of their dad. Afterwards, they will place the marble in this bag. Their memories will live on long after this day is over.

(Each child shares their memory, and places the marble in a hessian bag. These will accompany Jackson when he is interred in a council cemetery.)

Jackson, we will remember you. We will remember your stories.

We will remember.

Fire-inspired Narrative

The words in bold are 'fire' words.

To describe Kenzie's 92 years upon this Earth in the space of a handful of minutes is an impossible task; for hers was a life **bursting** with **vitality**, **passion**, **drive**, **adventure** and **fuelled** by the **desire** to make her community a better place for others.

You can tell a lot about a person by the way they **drive** a car. Kenzie: heavy right foot, changing gears while going around corners. In a **hurry** to get somewhere. Living life to the full!

It was during her pregnancy with Mary, way back in the early 1950s, that she learnt to drive, and discovered the immense **independence** it afforded her. Ten years ago, at the age of 82, she was caught **speeding** at Durranhill doing an **outrageous** 34mph! Kenzie was ordered to do a **speed-awareness** course. Some people might not admit to such a thing, but not Kenzie; she **thrived** on every minute of it! Being such a sociable person, she found the interaction with fellow **speedsters** totally **enlivening**.

Independence was a defining theme in her life, and this was **highlighted** by the fact she was still driving at 88.

Kenzie had **independence** modelled to her, for she was raised by a strong, single mother. Younger sister, Liz, was born four years after her, and despite the challenges in their lives, there was a richness to Kenzie's childhood. You could find her **swinging** a racket on the tennis court, writing letters to penfriends, and **cycling** all around Carlisle. As a youth, she was a gifted and disciplined **athlete** who found success representing the county in national **competitions**. So skilled was she that if the **war** hadn't come along, Kenzie would have almost certainly qualified for the **Olympics**! So why didn't she continue after the **war**? In a word: **boys**.

It was at the **cycle** repair shop where she met the love of her life. Love with Jack blossomed, and they fashioned a wonderful marriage of more than half a century. Their loving union **created** three children, Tracy, Jill and Jan.

Kenzie's mothering style reflected her nature. When her daughter Tracy had got into an **altercation** with another little girl, while they were **swinging** around concrete pillars outside Boots, Kenzie parked Jill in the pram just outside the shop. Then she **marched** in and **grabbed** Tracy and with **speed** in their step **hurried** all the way home. Upon seeing them, Jack asked 'did you forget something?' In her **haste**, she'd left Jill sitting in the pram outside Boots! Despite being abandoned, Jill says Kenzie was always there as a mum, wife and homemaker, and held the family together. There were moments when her **fiery** nature took **centre stage**, such as the time she poured a pot of tea over Jack's head! All those tea leaves! At least it was cold tea.

One time, she **hurled** a tea cup at Jill (anyone sensing a theme here?). Poor Jill ended up in **trouble** when it missed her!

***

If it hadn't been for the **spark** plugs in Gina's car failing, we wouldn't be here today. What seemed like a curse was a blessing in disguise. The road-rescue operative **warned** her it would be a seven-hour wait for a mobile mechanic to arrive. **Furious**, Gina ended the call. "Not **fast** enough," she **hissed** under her breath. On that Winter's afternoon, the **daylight** would soon end. According to Google Maps, there was a hotel just a mile away. On any other day, it wouldn't have seemed so far, but with the **threat** of a blizzard on the news there was no option. Donning her coat, she trudged over the hill and around the bend. As she drew closer to the old inn, Gina saw a **golden glow flickering** on the windowsill.

What she didn't know, what she couldn't have known, was that the first person she'd see inside would **light** a **flame** like no other. "It was **instant**," Gina recalled. "A **flare** was **kindled**. All that **anger** I'd felt half an hour earlier was gone."

Harry was driving home for Christmas and had stopped at The Goose Inn for a refreshment break. While waiting for the **cook** to **fry** him some chips, he'd settled down by the open **fire**, and **flicked** through the paper. As the only person in the snug that afternoon, it seemed natural to look up when the door opened. The chill breeze brought with it the most beautiful woman he'd even seen. Harry was never sure what **attracted** him first: that **bright red** hair or the **pop** of **freckles** on her cheeks or the **incendiary spark** in her eyes ready to **combust**.

Fire *warms*

Earth *stabilises*

Air *rises*

Water *merges*

Spirit *infuses*

Earth

"When we touch the earth mindfully
every step will bring peace and joy
to the world."
— Thich Nhat Hanh

As soon as we wear shoes or walk indoors, drive a car, sit at a laptop or mobile phone, we are disconnected from the Earth. And it is this disconnection, so prevalent in modern, civilised society, that has seen the rise of our egoic selves: where the focus is on one's self, rather than honouring our connection to the natural world, we desire more.

When we walk barefoot upon the Earth, we are instantly connected to the 'negative' ions. In this case, negative is a good thing. The modern life we live: microwaves, planes, Wi-Fi, phones, laptops, TV, and so on, contain and emit positive ions. These have a detrimental impact on our health.

Our glorious planet quickly absorbs these from our body the moment we are in touch with it: walking barefoot, hugging a tree, wild swimming, using an earthing sheet.

When was the last time you hugged a tree, or gathered a bouquet of wildflowers, or collected pebbles, or walked barefoot on the grass? Earth grounds us, and is the foothold of our stability.

*"The Earth is not just our environment.
We are the Earth and the Earth is us.
We have always been one with the Earth."*
— Thich Nhat Hanh

The earth element is seen in
- Soil, sand, gravel, clay, mud
- Rocks, stones, pebbles
- Crystals
- Caves
- Canyons
- Trees
- Forests
- Valleys, plains, meadows
- Gardens
- Parks

Earth
Ground
Give
Build
Heal

Earth In Ceremonial Work

Some of the following items work well when incorporating the earth element into our rituals and ceremonies.

Roots (including root vegetables like beetroot, potato, sweet potato, parsnip) symbolise stability and grounding.

Salt (such as Himalayan rock salt) is used for protection, and in rituals of romance and friendship.

Seeds can be used in various ways to symbolise new beginnings, fertility, strength, growth, prosperity.

Leaves work nicely in ceremonies, such as creating a love circle around a wedding couple, or as a blanket after an interment.

Flowers bring beauty to ritual and ceremony, and can be offered in blessings, cleansing and grounding.

Moss has a signature of stillness, and symbolises rapid growth, abundance, wealth and prosperity.

Acorns can be used whole, or dried as a coffee, and included to symbolise longevity, prosperity and protection.

Sand (such as desert, beach, river) is a symbol of resilience.

Chalk works well for casting circles, and for writing names.

Clay is a wonderful symbol of the earth element and can be used to make clay tiles, for example.

Mud, like clay, is quite a literal symbol of this element (can also be used for water). Use it for burying, cleansing, grounding.

Coins are used to symbolise abundance, and work well for career-change ceremonies or a lucky coin for a bride.

Moss Agate is used for grounding and to bring balance.

Emerald is called upon in ceremonies where truth is required. It can make a lovely oathing stone.

Ritual: *The Sweet Path Ahead*

Anita Moorjani asked: "What is the meaning of life? In other words, "Why are we here?" To eat chocolate, of course! Why else?" She said: "I know you think I'm kidding, but I'm actually not. Well…..ok, we're also here to watch glorious sunsets, to make love with our beloved, to laugh heartily, to love fearlessly, to live life fully and with abandon, and to do all the things that bring us joy."

Simon and Kali, as you move into your new life, free of past burdens, may you walk upon a sweet path. Take sustenance for this journey, and as you eat this chocolate let your whole being be infused by sweetness. Remember, we can grow just as easily through love and joy as anything else. You can choose this for yourselves.

Simon and Kali, please enjoy this chocolate.
(eat chocolate)

Bonding Ritual: *Sacred Bowl*

Around the world, in many cultures, sharing a drink with your beloved is a bonding ritual. Today's drink is Guinness, a nod to Leah's Irish heritage. May we remember that Guinness is brewed from barley, the grain used in love spells. It is associated with Venus and the element of Earth.

Chris, would you offer Leah a sip from the sacred bowl?
(sip)
Leah, would you offer Chris a sip?
(sip)
This sip is for all the love you've shared in the past, and the way your union has grown from strength to strength.

Chris, would you offer Leah a sip please?
(sip)
Leah, would you offer Chris a sip?
(sip)
This second sip is for right now: this moment. This magical portal between the past and the future; a threshold of renewal. This is the day you'll always remember as when you promised to *still choose each other.*

Chris, would you offer Leah a sip please?
(sip)
Leah, would you offer Chris a sip?
(sip)
This third sip is for all the love you've yet to experience, and the ways you'll love

yourselves and each other in a manner you can't yet even begin to imagine.

Wedding Ritual: *Rose Quartz Oathing Stone*
You both value that marriage is a journey of sharing, and to commit your hearts and lives in marriage is like signing something in stone. You've embraced the old-fashioned tradition of this with the intention that marriage keeps you committed. This rose quartz has been chosen as your oathing stone. Please hold the rose quartz while you offer your vows.
(Annabel and Joshua each hold the quartz during vow making)

Funerary Ritual: *The Love Stone*
In a moment, this rose-quartz love heart, the stone of love, will be passed to you. When you receive it, place the stone in the palm of your hand and imbue it with a prayer, wish or a blessing for Jasmine. Offer your love in whatever way is meaningful to you and your beliefs. The stone will naturally make its way back to the front, to Jasmine's mother, before the end of the ceremony. And then it will be placed with Jasmine as a holder of the love in this room today. *(pass the love stone)*

Love-Ceremony Ritual: *Growing Love*

As you continue to share your lives together, you'll be planting seeds each day. Let these be seeds of love, care, joy, fascination, adventure, compassion, respect, delight, birth, transformation, spontaneity, faith, truth and trust. Please take a moment to write down a list of five seeds you wish to plant, and then place it in your pocket.

(write lists)

For New Year's Eve or tomorrow morning, plant these seeds in the ground, and watch them germinate in your lives.

Funerary Ritual: *Finding Balance in the Bitter and Sweet; The Giving of Liquorice Allsorts*

Gabby loved Liquorice Allsorts! Liquorice symbolises balance, for it is a blend of sweet and bitter. Our time together today is bittersweet. We have so many lovely memories of Gabby that we'll hold close in our heart, and yet such sorrow at her parting.

(Funeral Director and Celebrant to pass sweets around during reflection music)

Ritual: *Pebble Blessing*

(Music to play during ritual)

Elsie is blessed to be growing up in a lovely home by the river. This home was built by an ancestor, and has been in the family since it was first resided in in 1904. Here she will play, laugh, sing, and create many happy memories with friends and family. The pebble you are holding is from the riverbed, and was gathered by Elsie, Martha and Martin especially for today's blessing.

In a moment, each of you will place the pebble you've been tasked to bless, and stick it here on this card where her name is written.

Later, after her name is written in pebbles, it will be framed by her parents as a loving legacy from today's ceremony. While the music plays, we respectfully ask that you refrain from any chatter so that we can all be fully present.
(*place pebbles to write her name*)

Funerary Ritual: *Manchester United Kit*
Charley 16, we offer you some Man U kit just in case you have any plans of running around naked! These clothes symbolise protection, and our wish for you is that wherever you may be, you are looked after well.
(*place kit on the coffin*)

Celebrant Note: This ritual could have been a fire-element ritual due to the red clothing, and because sport comes under this element. I've used it here because clothing gives us security (a symbol of the earth element.)

> *"Transport a handful of earth everyday*
> *and you will make a mountain."*
> — Confucius

Ritual: *The Hat*
In some traditions, a hat symbolises the connection between Heaven and Earth: humility, unity and impermanence. Today we leave this cap from Dalwhinnie Distillery, which was so loved by Roger, as a parting gift. We remember his love of travel, near and far, here and there, and acknowledge that by touching the coffin in the north, east, south and west. The west symbolises the horizon which we will also pass over. And then, remembering the ground he walked on, and his connection now to All That Is, we shall place this above.
(*Use the hat to touch the north, east, south and west sides of the coffin, then touch the ground, and then place on top of the coffin*)

*"Forget not that the earth delights
to feel your bare feet
and the winds long to play with your hair."*
— Khalil Gibran

Ritual: *Queen of Our Hearts*
Carlotta gave a piece of her heart to everyone, and was a fantastic friend. And now, we take with us a symbol of that love in the shape of a rose-quartz heart. Ava will pass you a heart, and April will tie a friendship bracelet around your wrist, if you like, during the reflection music.
(place rose-quartz love hearts in palms and tie on bracelets)

"Earth laughs in flowers."
— Ralph Waldo Emerson

Earth-inspired Narrative

Constance lived and led a beautifully bohemian lifestyle and was most at **home** wandering amongst the **flowers**, with a **companion dog** by her side, and a flair for seeing **value** in items of **history**. A free thinker, she wasn't **bound** by religion or dogma, choosing instead to create a life which suited her leanings and passionate pursuits. With the heart of an artist, she handcrafted her days around **nature**, **wildlife** and **animals**. Whatever Constance brought into her life, whether it was **flowers**, **pottery**, glassware, **clothing** or **artwork**, you can be sure they were chosen for colour and to bring interest and variety. Each of these reflected her personality: a woman who was at once astute, a tad naughty, **generous**, **formidable** and interesting.

When **organising** her funeral **arrangements** with nephew, Alex, she said "I'm going to do my funeral on the cheap!" Alex replied: "I'll take you out in a wheelie bin." Constance swiftly responded with "Put me out with the **garden** refuse. I'll make good **compost**!" Constance was right about that. To make a **good-quality compost** you need a mixture of **ingredients**; her whole being was **centred** on variety, **richness** and, in her own way, she **nourished** the world around her.

So in tune with **nature** was she, that Constance would open the door of the barn for migratory birds and let the swallows and martins in for the Summer. It was important to her that they had somewhere **safe** to **nest**. Never mind the mess, she'd get someone else to **clean** it up after breeding season was over. All that mattered was that they had a **home**.

The vibrant and life-giving **garden** was a testament to her **values**, with hedgehog **hotels** providing a **safe habitat** for them to rest, sleep and **hibernate** throughout the year. The honey bees had a **home**, too, with a **garden deliberately** left wild to make the most of the **abundant flora**. Every **mortal creature** was welcomed into her **Garden of Eden**. It didn't take long for Constance to dispense with the **lawn**, for she knew that it had no place if you wanted to encourage **wildlife**. And in her own way, day after day, she created a piece of paradise on **Earth**; a **haven** for insects, birds, small mammals, wildflowers, mosses and more.

***

When Layla trained as a **kinesiologist**, she was the only non-medically influenced person on the course. She **achieved** the second-highest grade. It was here, in her inner-city practice, that she was able to help others to align their emotional, mental and physical energies. From as early as her late twenties, Layla was fascinated by the power of **nutritional healing**, as well as the huge role the equilibrium between our mind and heart has on our **physical** healing. She understood that the language of the **body** always speaks the truth.

Blessed with so many natural talents and gifts, she **augmented** these with her studies and practice of hypnotherapy, **kinesiology**, **naturopathy** and **nutrition**. This extended to healing animals, and she absolutely loved working with children, particularly through Breath for Life, which was extremely important to her. Hers was a life lived in **service**: helping people to heal.

In every way, Layla was a healer as well as a spiritual teacher. Layla held dreams of **teaching** her **specialism** to others.

At the **crossroads** of life, she stepped into her **wisdom** to make people's lives **better**, to make the world a kinder place so more of us could walk in freedom and joy and **better health**. We're able to do this because Layla was a pioneer, and brave enough to step into her **strength** to **teach**, to **lead**, to **be of service**. She **paved** a **path** for all of us. Layla may not have seen herself as a pioneer, but she most certainly was.

Air

*"What is brought by the wind,
will be carried away by the wind."*
— Persian Proverb

Close your eyes and imagine the feel of a gentle breeze against your cheek. Air is the only element we can't see. It's an invisible energy that's all around us. From the merest hint of a breeze to catastrophic cyclones, the air in the world is constantly circulating far and wide. Although we can't see air, the moment we look outside we can sense her at play: the clouds scooting across the sky, smoke drifting upwards from chimney pots, the way leaves flutter by or trees sway, or whistling wind. Are you someone who embraces even the most brutal winds or are you, a bit like me, and detest blustery gusts?

We see the air element at work in:
Clouds
Breezes
Smoke
Hurricanes
Tornadoes
Cyclones
Sandstorms

Air
Observe
Breathe
Focus
Decide

Air is symbolised by:
- speech
- breath
- life
- communication
- thinking
- bells
- feathers
- incense
- chimes
- kites
- bubbles
- brooms
- swords
- affirmations
- pens
- quills
- books
- libraries
- radio/broadcasting
- magazines

Bubbles: Don't leave home without them. These work beautifully whether they're beginning, bonding or bereavement rituals. I *don't* use balloons for eco reasons. They're dangerous. Bubbles are environmentally and creature friendly.

Dandelion Seeds work well in any ceremony which requires wish making. You simply hold the dandelion clock in front of your mouth, then whisper your wish and blow the seeds away. They'll carry your wishes far and wide.

Whistles bring the energy of sound to a ceremony. They symbolise breath (air). You can use it to summon or invoke energies, disperse unwanted energy, or as a means of protection.

Wind Chimes shift energies and protect space. You can add messages to the chimes, and have the intentions sent out with the breeze.

Coloured Ribbons: Whether using for a handtying ritual, to bind spells or work with knots, ribbons bring beauty, colour and intention to a ceremony. They can be used in any type of ceremony.

Bells: In my local crematorium, the staff nicknamed me 'bell woman'. It's not like I ring bells a lot, but clearly no other celebrant in the area uses them. Bells work well in their association with air. They raise vibration, sound a change, and shift energy. I have several bells: Tibetan Prayer Bell; Witch's Bell; School Bell; Cow Bell; Singing Bowl; to name a few.

Besom: The Druid's Besom is often used by pagan celebrants at the end of a handfasting ceremony. The couple jump over it as a threshold symbol. Besoms can also be used to clear a circle or cast one.

Smoke carries intentions. You can use smoke from sage, candles, incense or charcoal.

Feathers are energy movers. I use feathers a lot in my ceremonial work. A white peacock feather works beautifully in the funeral of a baby as it is so light and gentle. I've also used them in an author blessingway ceremony, weddings, namings and other rites of passage. You can add further symbolism depending on the colour or type of feather.

Essential Oils can be introduced (as sprays or for anointing) to symbolise breathing in scent. Each oil has its own meaning.

Flute: a flute is just one of many instruments which can be incorporated into a ceremony to symbolise air. The sound of the flute carries the messages to faraway places.

Incense is something I burn before most of my ceremonies (with the exception of ceremonies in a crematorium). I aim to burn it about half an hour before the start of the ceremony (it has finished before we start) leaving a residual and beautiful scent. It cleanses space and raises the energy of any ceremonial space. My preference is Nag Champa (original or rose).

Kite: This can serve in a similar way to balloons but without the catastrophic effect they have on wildlife. Carry your messages high to the sky.

Quill: While considered old fashioned, they are the perfect way to symbolise wisdom. Use them for any rituals emphasising knowledge, writing, communication, ideas.

Wand: Some elemental workers use the wand to symbolise fire. I use them for air. It is a focus and spell caster.

"With your fragrance in the air,
I give my love to the wind."
— Rumi

In Ceremonial Work

Love Circle

It is an ancient love charm to scatter rose petals around the feet of a couple on their wedding day. Mike and Felicity, these petals form a circle around you, this shall be your sacred space in which you'll make your vows, pledges and promises to each other.

(scatter petals)

You can use all types: flowers, leaves and so on to create a circle.

- Roses
- Lavender
- Delphinium
- Sunflowers
- Eucalyptus leaves
- Willow leaves
- Pine needles
- Calendula petals
- Rosemary twigs

Communal Gift: *Two Words*

As their friends and family, you are Lizi and Ben's community. You are their people: the ones they'll turn to, time and time again, during happy moments and in seasons of sadness. They count on you to offer solace, fun, a listening ear, and an open heart.

In a moment, I'll call out a series of words, just two at a time. After each set of two words, your job—your gift to this couple, if you like—is to call back with just one of the words! There's no right or wrong answer. Ready? Big voices!

Rugby or reading?
Walking or running?
Pub lunch or picnic?
Snow or sunshine?
Humour or creativity?
Theatre or sport?
Joy or adventure?
BBQ or dog walk?
Friends or family?

"With every breath, I plant the seeds of devotion,
I am a farmer of the heart. "
— Rumi

Origami
In Japanese mythology, the wings of the crane carried souls up to heaven. In origami, the folded crane (Orizuru) can be used to symbolise sending a message to heaven. A swan can be made to contain a message (or ashes) to float down a stream.

Crossing the Threshold
This ceremony is divided into two distinct sections: releasing the past, which you've done; and, here in the magic of the present moment, calling out to the future with intentions.

Ritual: *Sage Cleansing*
This is the moment where we cleanse the space of all energies which no longer belong here with you, Sindy, or you, Karl.

We let them fly off in the invisible energy of the wind.
(Waft sage incense around the ceremonial space for a moment)

Ritual: *Bell Ringing*
The ringing of this bell marks crossing the threshold between those two purposes.
(Veronika to ring the bell three times)

Relationship Healing Ritual: *The Stone of Truth*

Sindy and Karl, there are so many positives to your relationship. At the foundation is deep love.

The most important aspect of a relationship is communication, and for this to come from a place of honesty, care, kindness and respect. Today, we draw upon the energies of the stone, Shattuckite. It will also help you to connect with your higher self, and if you believe in them, past lives. First and foremost, it will help you connect to universal wisdom. It acts as a conduit, activating the throat and third-eye chakras.

You can also consider this as the stone of portals and doorways connecting you to other realms, and the opening of communication channels.

As you both take turns in holding this Stone of Truth, allow it to inspire truthfulness in the words you speak, and in how you live your lives. If there have been wounds to your heart from the other person's hurtful words, this stone will allow you to see beyond and to mend. Karl, will you hold the stone first? *(holds stone)*

Are you willing to recognise the truth within, and to identify the areas in your relationship where you can align to a Higher Truth?   *(I am)*

Sindy, will you hold the stone now?
(holds stone)
Are you willing to step into self-awareness and self-responsibility, and use these as tools for truthtelling?
(I am)

Sindy, with this stone, shattuckite, in one hand, and your other hand on Karl's heart, please look into his eyes and offer forgiveness. This is a moment to repair all previous hurts. You've both asked to reboot this relationship. In this moment of truth, drop an anchor of trust.

Are you willing to let Karl know that you forgive him, and yourself, for all past actions which knowingly or unknowingly, created hurt or pain?
(Sindy answers)

Please repeat after me: "Karl, with this hand on the stone of truth, and this hand on your heart, I fully free you from all untruths and hurts. I forgive you, and I let all hurts go."
(hand on stone, and hand on heart)

Karl, with this stone, shattuckite, in one hand, and your other hand on Sindy's heart, please look into her eyes and offer forgiveness. This is a moment to repair all previous hurts. You've both asked to recharge this relationship. In this moment of truth, drop an anchor of trust.

Karl, are you willing to let Sindy know that you forgive her, and yourself, for all past actions which knowingly or unknowingly, created hurt or pain?
(Karl answers)

Please repeat after me, if you're willing, "Sindy, with this hand on the stone of truth, and this hand on your heart, I fully free you from all untruths and hurts. I forgive you, and I let all hurts go."
(hand on stone, and hand on heart)

Naming Ritual: *The Ancestral Name*
Alfred, as a guardian to the surname Mallinson, would you please pass it down the family line to Stacey by whispering the name, Mallinson, in her ear?
(whispers Mallinson into Stacey's ear) Thank you.

This next ritual honours the name of a baby who died in infancy.

Funerary Ritual: *Writing Her Name*
Maryanne, you are welcome to pick up the feather, and write Ophelia's name in the air three times.
(writes her name with white peacock feather)
Thank you.

Naming Ritual: *Community Blessing*
Today we've heard how the naming of people is a magical art. All names are composed of letters, and each letter carries a numerical or spiritual vibration. Abracadabra is also a magical word as it shows us the power to create our own reality. In really loud voices, would each of you repeat after me: *Abracadabra ~ we name you Maximus!*
Repeat: Abracadabra ~ we name you Maximus!

Vow-Renewal Ritual: *The Wand of Wonderful New Beginnings*
Kitty, you have your wand here today. As we bring this ceremony to a close, will you and Levi cast a spell? Speak your words of intention now.
(wave the wand and affirm)

Marriage-Preparation Ritual: *The Knot of Trust*
Next year you'll be tying the knot at your wedding ceremony. Until that day arrives, put your trust in the here and now. Honour that you're both strong people and that you can define your life free of other people's opinions. Choose the path ahead of you.

Please take this cord and tie a knot. This is the knot of trust. If you work together, you can create a double knot. When you've done so, place it in this water.
(tie the knot and place it in water)
Water makes the knot tighter.

Please hold each other's hands and look into each other's eyes, and if you're willing, will you repeat after me:
"Vernon, I trust you."
"Julia, I trust you."

Funerary Ritual: *Three Carnations*

We entered into this chapel today to the hymn The Old Rugged Cross. And as we draw near to the end of this ceremony, we reflect again on the cross. According to legend, carnations grew from Mary's tears as she watched her son, Jesus, carry the cross. And for this reason, carnations are associated with a mother's pure love.

And so today, we place three pink carnations with Carrie: a gift from each of her beloved children, as a symbol of gratitude for all her years of devoted mothering. Derek, will you now gift the carnations to your Mam?
(place three carnations)

Naming-Ceremony Ritual: *Seed Bomb*

Have a large bowl of native wildflower seeds and another bowl of clay. Invite guests to make seeds bombs that they can take home and plant to grow alongside the child. In your narrative, talk about the flowers in the mix and their symbolism.

Leaf Butterfly
You will need:
- Sticks
- Chalk Pens
- Leaves

Each guest or mourner paints leaves. A leaf is attached to either side of a small stick so it looks like a butterfly. These leaf butterflies can have the person's name written on them. (e.g. naming ceremony, funeral ceremony)

Wedding Ritual: *Anointing*
Anointing is a sacred ritual. Dane you've chosen sandalwood, and Ruth you've chosen rose. Sandalwood oil is used for its ability to carry one's intention to the divine. Rose is for the heart, and strengthens the heart chakra. These have been blended together.
(Anoint wrists with a pentagram)

Dane, could you please close your eyes and allow your heart to fill with the most beautiful intentions for this marriage?

Ruth, could you please close your eyes and allow your heart to fill with the most beautiful intentions for this marriage?

(Stillborn) Funerary Ritual: *Pink Gerbera Blessing*

Caitlin, we offer you this gerbera for innocence, ivy for our attachment to you, and rosemary so that we always remember.

(*touch the coffin three times with a posy of gerbera, ivy and rosemary*)

Funerary Ritual: *Bubbles of Release*

Roo recalls how much his Mam loved to see bubbles blowing on the breeze. Last year, during a BBQ, there was a bubble machine blowing them all about the garden and she could see them floating past her bedroom window. Lexie said it reminded her of how much Roo loved them when he was a child.

Committal

Lexie, this Earthly world is no longer your home, and you are now free from all pain. We offer your mortal physical body to the sacred flame for transformation. We do so with immense love, respect and tenderness. Return to the Dream Maker, and be at peace.

Blow Bubbles

These bubbles are for you, Lexie. *Fly free.*
(*blow bubbles over coffin*)

Ritual: *The Gift of Heather*
Eilidh, as symbolic of your Scottish roots, we brush this sprig of heather as a reminder that despite the challenges of your early life, and the ongoing passage of time, you continued to grow and blossom. And just as heather in the wild brings colour to the dreary browns of the landscape, you too brought colour to the lives of all those around you. Thank you, Eilidh.
We honour you.
We respect you.
We love you.
(*brush pink heather back and forth across the coffin and place it by her photo*)

Funerary Ritual: *Memory Card*
We remember Dexter's passion for football. There won't be any yellow or red cards issued today. However, during the next piece of music, you're welcome to write a message to or about Dexter. You'll find pens and cards at the end of each pew. Please pass them along to each other. You might like to write one positive word which makes you think of Dexter or perhaps something along the lines of "I remember when..." followed by your favourite memory.

At the end of the ceremony, on your way out, please place the cards up here and leave the pens in the other basket. These cards will be kept by Dexter's family.

(*cards passed around and filled in while music plays*)

This full chapel is evidence of how many lives Dexter touched, the kindness given, and friendships woven across this town and further afield.

Funerary Ritual: *The Full-time Whistle*

Gordon, with the blowing of this whistle, we declare full time. We wish you a safe journey.

(blow the whistle three times)

Ritual: *Fairy Dust*

You will need:

- Glitter
- Cornflour
- Lavender blossoms

Using biodegradable glitter (made from a cellulose of eucalyptus trees, and decomposes naturally), cornflower and chosen ground blossoms, mix together, and create Fairy Dust. I often use this in my naming ceremonies.

Fairy dust can be:

- Strewn around the ceremonial space
- A path of new beginnings, accompanied by fairies.

It can be used in namings, funerals, weddings and other rites of passage.

Prayer Flags

- Squares of calico 20cm x 20cm
- Fabric pens

Invite mourners to create images or write a prayer, wish or a blessing for the child. The flags can either be strung up at the ceremony or gathered together for the family to hang up at home or in the garden.

"Thoughts come and go like leaves in the wind, but the core of consciousness is forever."
— Deepak Chopra

Air-inspired Narrative

Memories of Dave

If Dave was standing here, he'd start with "All I'm gonna **say**…" before dispensing his wisdom. Dave's mother would often **say** that he'd be late for his own funeral! And yet, here he is: dead on time. Whether you knew Dave from agriculture and farming, or **dealing**, one thing we all share in common is that we're here to **remember** a loveable rogue. Despite having friends all over the country, and a tendency to stop by each of their homes for a couple of hours at a time as he drove the length and breadth of the land, he was actually a rather quiet, private man whose best bit of advice was "Never **tell** anyone what you've got!"

It is **said** that one man's rubbish is another man's treasure. But if you got it from our Dave the Dealer it was probably still rubbish! The only difference was that he'd convince you it was a real treasure. Odds were high that he'd probably sold you something before he'd even bought it himself. Dave could **talk** his way into or out of absolutely anything; indeed, he was a man who'd perfected the art of **patter**.

Dave could eye up a pile of scrap, and not only see something, he'd see top dollar. *Expensive* scrap. And not surprisingly, even though he has lots of **friends**, there's the odd enemy lurking among the rust.

***

It was only natural that Felix and Andie's **meeting** would involve **words**. Felix had long worked in **broadcasting** and Andie's career change to **journalist** meant that sooner or later their circles would collide.

What neither of them would ever have **guessed** was that they'd **meet** on a day off. The **storm** which **swept** through the city had caused a **power outage** in their suburbs. Without heating, it seemed a preferable **option** to **travel** to the next town and seek out a place to keep warm. They'd even caught the same **train** that afternoon. Andie often headed into Bluebell **Bookshop** when she wanted a quiet afternoon, and there she'd sit in the corner, her **curiosity refreshed** by **studying** the **books** on the shelves.

For the past three years she'd **balanced** her **journalism** degree with **studies** in Estonian.

Immersed in the foreign-languages section, the **scent** of a distinctive aftershave **distracted** her. What was that? Rosehip? Elderberry? Sage? Patchouli? As soon as she looked up, the whole world changed. When Felix smiled at her, Andie instantly **recognised** him from his Friday night **news** show. "Hi," he **said**. "Hey," she **replied**.

Water

*"In one drop of water are found
all the secrets of all the oceans."*
— Khalil Gibran

There's something so nourishing about being by a calming body of water: the gentle lap of waves coming into a secluded and sheltered bay; the ripples on a pond; a babbling brook; sipping water from an ancient spring; walking in gentle rain; being barefoot on dew-covered grass. Water refreshes, cleanses, heals. We call upon water to rejuvenate.

Water is seen in:
Well
Spring
Pond
Lake
Ocean
River
Mist
Fog
Rain
Hail
Snow

The water element symbolises deep feelings, healing, psychic abilities, intuition, self-healing, reflection.

Coral is used for protection rituals.

Hagstones (stones which have holes in them that have occurred naturally) are used for connecting Spiritside.

Driftwood is beautiful to use as a reminder of travelling far from home, about change, and transformation.

Seaglass: smoothed by the sea, this is also used for transformation.

Seaweed is used in ceremony to symbolise the water element, abundance, going with the flow.

Seashells are used for wisdom and empowerment.

Starfish are used in ceremonies for new beginnings and for protection.

Sand Dollar: These work well in ceremonies where we seek wholeness and wellbeing for our client. It is associated with prosperity.

Water comes in many forms, such as rain water, sea water, river water. It can be used in libations and sprays, for healing, protection and rejuvenation.

Flower Water and **Moon Water** are those which you create and charge by combining flowers (or herbs) with spring or rain water. Moon water is charged under a New or Full Moon. I use it in a variety of ceremonies for healing, hope, kindness and reasons connected to the element of the zodiac sign the Moon was in at the time.

Mirror: Mirrors can be used in any type of ceremony where you are wishing to symbolise reflection, protection or to show the energy of water through 'stillness'. I've used it in weddings, vow renewals, namings and funerals.

Pearls symbolise healing and are used in rituals of transformation.

Bowl: As a bowl represents 'holding' and nurturing, it works nicely for reminding us about the cycles of life and rebirth. You can use it to hold water for sprinkling, libation or drinking.

Cauldron: Though I am more inclined to use this with Wiccan clients, it can be used in any ceremony where we wish to bring in the energies of the Divine Feminine.

Chalice: also connected with femininity, the chalice holds water, and works beautifully in bonding and healing rituals.

Water
Cry
Cleanse
Release
Flow

"Water is the mirror of nature."

- Francis of Assisi

Water in Rituals & Ceremonies

Ripple Effect: pebbles dropped into water to show the changes that have happened because of that person.

Flower Water
Using edible flowers only, wash the petals, and place in a pan with a small amount of spring water. Simmer for a short time until they have wilted. Strain and refrigerate the liquid. Each flower has its own symbolism. This water can be used for drinking, libation, sprays or sprinkling.

Celebrant Note: *Pumice*
Although pumice could fall under the element of fire due to it being made of lava, or air because of frothy gas from which it was formed, due to its lightness, it works nicely for the water element, too, as per the next ritual.

Healing Ritual: *Staying Afloat*
Grace, you've walked the path of depression for several years now. Jayne and Amelia have held space for you, been there in your darkest hours, and continue to be your guardians on Earth.

This ritual offers cleansing and nourishment.

Amelia, will you please place the bowl at Grace's feet?
(*places bowl*)

Jayne, will you now add the pumice?
(*places pumice*)

Amelia and Jayne, will you now pour in these two jugs of warm water?
(*pours water*)

Grace, take note of how the pumice is rising to the surface. We know that you've often felt like you're drowning in sorrow. Baby Ebony's death changed your life. We know that. We acknowledge your deep well of grief.

When you're ready, place one foot into the bowl.
(*places foot*)
Jayne will now use the pumice to slough away any negative energy that doesn't belong to you.
(*sloughs heel*)

Whatever needs to go, be gone.
Whatever needs to stay, you're welcome.

When you're ready, place the other foot into the bowl.
(*places foot*)
Amelia will now use the pumice to slough away any negative energy that doesn't belong to you.
(*sloughs heel*)
Whatever needs to go, be gone.
Whatever needs to stay, you're welcome.

Amelia will now carry this water away and offer it to Mother Earth. Let this planet absorb your pain, Grace. Let the Earth be a safe place for you to walk. We are here for you.

Jayne will now dry your feet and Amelia will massage them with this mix of essential oils to heal your heartache: lavender, ylang ylang and chamomile. Asher will play the harp during the massage. Feel free to close your eyes.
(*massage feet*)

Funerary Ritual: *Willow Love Tree*
Melody spent many happy hours playing with her dollies and laughing under the corkscrew willow tree in their garden. Jock and Vi have brought several branches from that tree here today and have placed them in this tall vase. While the reflection music plays, please write

your name on these willow-leaf cards and then place it on one of the branches.
(*writing names and placing them on branches*)

Coffin-Blessing Water
Some of the ways I've used water to bless a coffin, are with:

- Lavender
- Iris
- Rosemary
- Salt (to symbolise our tears)
- Honey (friendship)
- Rose
- Eucalyptus
- Chakra glass
- Lily of the Valley
- Carnation
- Sunflower
- Yarrow
- Holly
- Veronica
- Cypress
- Lily
- Alstromeria
- Sage
- Wild Mint
- Jasmine
- Honeysuckle

Iris-Water Blessing

The symbolism of the iris flower is one of hope and is considered a connection between this world and the next. This flower shall be used as we say goodbye to Iris.

(Stir water three times with the iris, then sprinkle iris water on the coffin)
Thank you Iris for your love.
(iris-water blessing)
Thank you for your care.
(iris-water blessing)
Thank you for being uniquely you.
(iris-water blessing)

Interment of Ashes Funerary Ritual:
Gifts from the Sea

Mark, today we leave you with four gifts:
This seawater symbolises our emotions, and the salty tears shed at your passing. Angela, as Mark's sister, will you pour this libation of sea water?
(Angela pours sea water into interment space)

This shell symbolises home and family. Jan, as Mark's sister, would you place this shell here?
(Jan places the shell)

This sand from the beach symbolises the shifting sands of time, and how nothing stays the same. Danny will you sprinkle sand here? (*Danny sprinkles sea sand*)

And finally, we add driftwood. Mark, it symbolises that you left your roots and crossed the seas. You weren't, at any point, restrained by your roots. Travel enhanced you. Like driftwood, you were tumbled and tossed and stripped away to reveal the true essence of you. You never betrayed your roots but simply went with the flow, floating through life and moving where the tides carried you.

Ivy, would you please add this final gift? (*Ivy places driftwood*)
Mark, you were bleached by the Sun.
Like driftwood, you were whittled by the rubbing of sand over time. Stained by the salt, this preservation will keep you in our memories for as long as the sea keeps kissing the shoreline. Be at peace, now.

Elopement Ritual: *Sacred Handwashing*
(bowl filled with warm water, lavender, rose petals and rosemary)

This day is one where you acknowledge that you are with the person who fills your heart. Whatever challenges may have existed, your love is greater.

Before adorning your hands with wedding rings, we draw upon an ancient tradition of matrimonial handwashing. In some religions, cleanliness is next to Godliness.

Water brings forgiveness.
Forgiveness is release.
Release offers healing.

Free each other from any and all past misunderstandings. Begin anew.

Emily, you may wash Karen's hands.

Karen, you may wash Emily's hands.
(Wash each other's hands)
Allowing yourselves to have your hands dried by each other signifies your vulnerability.

To create true intimacy in your marriage, based on love and compassion, you will need courage.

Emily, you may dry Karen's hands.
(dry hands)
Karen, you may dry Emily's hands.
(dry hands)

Emily and Karen, are you ready to begin your married life with grace and compassion?
(yes)

The Mirror of Marriage: *Into Me See*
Clyde and Chris, to truly know, love and trust another, it is important to know oneself. Looking into a mirror allows you to see yourself in truth. The handheld mirror is symbolic of the truths to be found when we look within. The true meaning of intimacy is: into me see. You know what this feels like: when your hearts are fully connected, you see into who the other really is, and they see into you. Clyde and Chris, not only do you share your lives, but you share your hearts. This is true intimacy.

Clyde, please hold and look into the mirror.
(looks in mirror)

Please repeat after me: "I see you Clyde. I see your light and I see your shadow."

Now, show Chris her reflection.
Please repeat after me: "I see you Chris. By seeing you, I see me. I see your light and I see your shadow."

Chris, please hold and look into the mirror.
(*looks in mirror*)
Please repeat after me: "I see you, Chris. I see your light and I see your shadow."

Now, show Clyde his reflection.
Please repeat after me: "I see you, Clyde. By seeing you, I see me. I see your light and I see your shadow."

You cannot hide from the deeper reflections of the soul and mind, the honesty of who you are or who you want to be. To love another well you must be true to yourselves. In doing so you can realise and reveal the better part of your being.

As a couple you can look within and at each other, helping to raise conscious awareness and personal understanding. Understanding yourselves and each other invites compassion, patience, consideration and thoughtfulness, strengthening the loving bonds of union further.

Naming Ritual: *Elemental Circle*
Saskia's Guide Parents will each bring one of the four elements from the altar, and walk around this family once, before returning them.
Hedy, carry the candle to represent fire
Rob, carry the quartz to represent earth
Alix, carry the feather to represent air
Tommy, carry the spring water to represent the water element

As Guide Parents, you have surrounded this family with the elements of life: fire, earth, air and water. These symbolise passion, stability, clear thinking and emotional wellbeing.

(Note: The family were atheist, so in this case they didn't wish for any reference to the fifth element)

Water-inspired Narrative

When you take a gap year after finishing secondary school, it's with the intention of separating childhood from adulthood responsibilities. You're crossing a threshold. Rebecca's dream to become a community **nurse** was firmly on the horizon. But first, a year of **sailing** to three countries. In Costa Rica, she found her first paid work: **cleaning yachts** for the rich and famous. The **coastline** looked beautiful as the **tides** rolled in. Lost in her **imagination**, **dreaming** of playing in **puddles** and walking barefoot on **beaches**, she envisaged her next day off as a carefree way to get to know this beautiful place. A **splash** in her bucket brought her back to reality. Six feet, blond and with 'the best smile ever', Marcus hummed a tune and then said "Hey there. I've been asked by the **skipper** to help you. I'm Marcus. You're from England, too, right?" Right from that moment, Rebecca wondered how it was possible to feel like you've known someone forever. Their work soon turned to laughter as they **splashed** each other, pretending to **douse** the deck with **water** but **soaking** each other while rubbing it down with a **sponge**.

Spirit

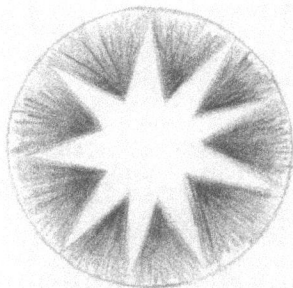

"External phenomena appear within space,
remain within space
and disappear within space again.
Is there any place where
earth, water, fire and wind
can go that is outside space?"
— Tulku Urgyen Rinpoche

Spirit
Listen
Know
Be Still

This element is often excluded (or unknown) when we talk of elements. If you're non-religious, atheist or humanist, you can use this element's energy in a secular way: simply think of the sky and how unlimited and unbounded it is.

If you're open to a more expansive or supernatural way of thinking and living, Spirit is the element which, in one sense, moves us away from the four elements, and yet it originates and includes them. Without Spirit, we wouldn't have fire's passion, earth's stability, air's lightness and water's flow. All the life that's contained within the other four elements owes its existence to the stillness of Spirit. *Quintessence* was how the medieval alchemists of old described the stars and galaxies in the heavens.

Spirit is symbolised by:
Mystery
Self-awareness
Wholeness
Unity
Ascension
Harmony

Circle: Of all the symbols, the circle is quite possibly one of the best for honouring Spirit. There is no beginning and no end. Use it for protection.

Spiral: Often used to symbolise our growing spiritual nature, and how we evolve from one level of divine consciousness to the next.

Wheel: Pagans understand this through the Wheel of the Year. It shows us the repetition of cycles.

Cords: Can be included to show connection and creation. Used in handfasting ceremonies for the handtying ritual. We can use cords in many types of ceremonies.

Infinity: Another symbol of cycles and the ongoing connection between all things.

Clear quartz: This has a particular resonance with Spirit and is often used for protection, healing and connection.

World Tree: Symbolises the link between realms. Used in ceremonies for protection and longevity.

Ritual: *Angel Canopy Orchid Essence*
As we lead into our last collective expression of farewell, this orchid essence, called Angel Canopy, shall be sprayed around the coffin. It acts as a balm in grief, and offers a path of grace.
(Spray angel-canopy essence)

Committal
Zeke, we tenderly, lovingly and with deep reverence offer your mortal physical body to the sacred flame of transformation. Return to the Breathmaker and the Angels.
(Touch the coffin, and then invite Sally [Zeke's wife] to come and touch it with me)

Blessing: *Calling All Angels*
Zeke, the Light of the Angels surrounds you.
May the Love of all the Angels enfold you.
May the Power of Angelic Life protect you.

May the Presence of All Angels watch over you.
Zeke, wherever you are, the Angels are. There is peace.
Blessed Be.
(The above blessing was adapted from the Unity Prayer)

Cutting Cords

There are many cords, connections and karmic ties we weave into and out of our lives. For better and for worse, they can shape us but they can also blind our way and tug us in directions which aren't for our higher purpose.

Today is an opportunity to consciously dissolve, release and cut cords which have outlived their time. It's as easy as it's difficult. The change can happen in an instance. The choice is yours.

Josh, are you ready to energetically dissolve old vows and ties? *(yes)*

You might like to close your eyes and bring to mind those people (whether known or unknown) with whom you'd like to cut cords.

As you do so, thank them for the opportunities they've given you to grow, learn and heal. In your mind and from your heart, release them.

When you're ready, take a ribbon from the bowl for each person you're cutting ties with. Hold one end close to your heart, and I'll take the other end for you and stand in as a proxy.

Josh, you'll now symbolically cut the cord for each set of vows or promises with people who no longer serve you.
(cut the cord/s with scissors)

(Place either side of the cut cords into different bowls.)
This side of the cord, the one closest to you, symbolises your boundaries and place in this world, and in the present moment. The other side of the cord is no longer connected to you. It is released to the person concerned, and is theirs and theirs alone.

And Kate, are you ready to energetically dissolve old vows and ties? *(yes)*

You might like to close your eyes and bring to mind those people (whether known or unknown) with whom you'd like to cut cords.

As you do so, thank them for the opportunities they've given you to grow, learn and heal. In your mind and from your heart, release them.

When you're ready, take a ribbon from the bowl for each person you're cutting ties with. Hold one end close to your heart, and I'll take the other end for you and stand in as a proxy for each person.

Kate, you'll now symbolically cut the cord for each set of vows or promises with people who no longer serve you.
(cut the cord/s with scissors)
(Place either side of the cut cords into different bowls.)
This side of the cord, the one closest to you, symbolises your boundaries and place in this world, and in the present moment. The other side of the cord is no longer connected to you. It is released to the person concerned and is theirs and theirs alone.

Ritual: *Ivy Circle*
Ani and Simon, Could you each choose two crystal wands, and then place them to mark four points in a circle in which you'll stand?
(place four crystals down)

This is:
A circle of *love*
A circle of *magic*
A circle of *protection*

We call on the energies of selenite today to bring forth the Light of Spirit, and to bring balance between light and matter.

Tourmaline will bring commitment, emotional stability, joy and contentment to your choices. It is known as the receptive stone, and brings spiritual and mystical energies.

Rose quartz is for aligning the heart, the place within our body where we consciously feel. Known as the stone of universal love, it teaches us about self-love, platonic love, romantic love, and unconditional love. This stone magnifies what is already in your heart. Amethyst is known for its high vibrational frequency. May each of you be open to receiving higher wisdom, divine guidance, as well as listening to your intuitive voice within.

As you stand at this threshold, free of the past, let us create another energetic circle around you. These lengths of ivy are a symbol of fidelity. Ivy shows us about interconnectedness

and intertwining, and the twists and turns of long-lasting connections and bonds.
(Place ivy around the circle)

> *"Silence is the altar of Spirit.*
> *Where motion ceases,*
> *Spirit beings to manifest."*
> – Paramahansa Yogananda

Celebrant Note: The following ritual could go under air, because it is a scent, however because of the person's spiritual belief in angels, I included it under Spirit.

Funerary Ritual: *The Scent of Remembrance*
Nellie and Mara will walk up and down the aisle to spray a fine mist of Rose Oil as we consciously invoke the energy of the angels that are accompanying Georgina now, and also to allow us to be at peace with her new adventure: the greatest journey of all. *(While they are walking up the aisle, say the following words:)*

As you breathe in the scent of the rose, think of Georgina, and remember her for: beauty, elegance, strength, vibrancy, courage, health, brightness, light, passion.

Raise your hand if you will remember Georgina for:

♥Her love of burning incense?

♥Or the Angel perfume that she never went without?

♥Raise your hand if you will remember Georgina for her playful romps at the park with her neurotic Dalmatian, Daisy?

♥Who among you will always remember her for her love of angels?

♥Raise your hand if you were aware of Georgina's passion for red roses?

♥Is anyone here aware of her matchmaking skills?

♥Raise your hand if you ever played squash with her?

♥Or if you ran 10km twice a week with Georgina?

♥Raise your hand if Georgina was your friend?

♥Perhaps she was your health-care provider? Raise your hand.

♥Can you raise your hand if she was your grandmother?

♥If Georgina was your sister?
♥Raise your hand if Georgina was your mother.

Funerary Ritual: *Angel Garland Blessing*
This ball of thread is silver, the colour of peace and emotional balance. We draw on silver now as an anchor during this time of immense grief and heartache.

In a moment, we shall each thread one of these paper angels to the one before it until we've created a garland. Tyson and Jenny will then wrap the garland around Anushka's coffin.
(*Mourners thread their angel*)
Baby girl, you never had the chance to breathe in the air of this Earth or walk alongside your mammy and daddy. They have breathed you into their hearts. They've held you and cuddled you with their never-ending love. And now, sweet, sweet girl, you are wrapped in the arms of angels. May you dance amongst the starlit Universe.

We shall now walk from this chapel, with Anushka, on her final journey. Tyson and Jenny will lead the way as we head to the baby burial ground.

*"A great silent space holds
all of nature in its embrace.
It also holds you."*
— Eckhart Tolle

Spirit-inspired Narrative

What you may not know about Gene is that he was a deeply **spiritual** man. This **reverence** was **inspired** by the years when he lived in Sheffield, and he'd attend philosophy classes. Gene believed in a **Great Being**, and was constantly searching for a **higher meaning** to life. By the late 1970s, he'd started visiting Findhorn, the **spiritual retreat** centre in the far north of Scotland. He'd stay for a week at a time, devoting himself to the spiritual practice of meditation. And, perhaps, it was this connection to **something greater** which allowed him to be so relaxed and accepting of his illness in recent times.

***

Transformation doesn't knock on our door lightly. And it certainly didn't for Millie. Her days, indeed her life, were built upon beliefs in **karma**; that is, what you sow, you shall reap ~ as well, understanding the **Higher Self**, and that we're here on this Earth to experience and learn. In her lifetime, she tried to heal humanity one person at a time.

Possessed of an expansive, generous and gracious heart, she wholeheartedly believed in love. Millie came to understand that to heal humanity we each need to **raise our vibration**, and to take responsibility for our thoughts and feelings. Perhaps Millie's greatest desire of all was to be **connected to her Creator**. For her, this was a path of **stillness** and **silence**. Always opening to this **divine connection**, she became aware, at some point, that it is within the small daily rituals of life, when we live mindfully and consciously, that we find such a relationship.

***

Everyone who'd ever seen him in St Matthew's Boys' Choir knew he'd be destined for **monastic** life. Brother Morris lived in the **monastery** for his whole adult life. Each day was bookended by **prayer**. If there was one thing people always said about him, it was that he was the calmest and kindest **soul** they'd ever met. Other brothers often sought his advice, but Morris, well, his answer to everything was to sit in **stillness** and welcome in the **silence**.

Reflecting on the Elements

Fire for *desire*
Earth for *grounding*
Air for *thinking*
Water for *feeling*
Spirit for *being*

When you have a solid understanding of the qualities of each element, you are able to work naturally and authentically in using each one to raise the energy of intention in your ceremonies.

Fire

When considering this element, think about the way fire illuminates and energises. It ignites. It moves us to action.

Write down five things which inspire you and 'fire' you up?

1.

2.

3.

4.

5.

Earth

The earth element teaches us about building, healing, nourishing, growing and grounding. It is solid. It encourages us to seek comfort.

Write down five things which ground you and give you a sense of solidity, structure and security?

1.

2.

3.

4.

5.

Air
The air element is about breathing, thinking, observing, communication, learning and focus.

Identify your thinking and learning style, and your sense of how you breathe.

1.

2.

3.

4.

5.

Water

The water element symbolises letting go, flowing, adapting, washing away, feeling and cleansing.

What are five ways you express your emotions and feel nourished? Identify times you've cleansed your pain.

1.

2.

3.

4.

5.

Spirit
The spirit element is our connection to All That Is.

In what ways do you consciously connect to this? How does Spirit show up in your life?

1.

2.

3.

4.

5.

Elemental Relationships

As an astrologer, my mother often talked about how the elements impacted each other and it has stayed with me over the years. The relationship between them can be helpful and harmonious or challenging and complicated. There's no 'good' and 'bad' element or elemental relationship. Like anything in life, when taken to extremes, it can cause problems and devastation. Generally speaking, water and earth elements work well together, and fire and air can be compatible, too.

Let's look closer:

Water *drowns* fire.
Fire brings water to the *boil*. It can form *steam*, *fog* and *mist*.

Water *nourishes* earth. And yet…she *floods*, *erodes* and *waterlogs* the earth. Water *erodes*. Earth can *contain* water.

Water *dissolves* metals when combined with air.
Air is a *container* for water: clouds, storms, humidity and hurricanes.

Air can turn earth into a dustbowl and *dry* it
out. Earth can stay *strong* in cruel winds.
Fire can *turn* air into smoke and steam. Air,
when breathed into fire, makes it *volatile* and
wild. Too much air *extinguishes* a flame.

Fire *reshapes* earth into crystals. Fire *scorches*
the earth, and from that, new life grows. Earth
extinguishes fire.

Fire to *move*
Earth to *be*
Air to *think*
Water to *feel*
Spirit to *exist*

Elemental Vocabulary

Enriching your vocabulary of the elements will enhance your script writing. Here are some examples.

Fire-Element Words
Anger, determined, dramatic, impulsive, blast, fiery, edgy, open, fun, courage, willpower, power, spark, light, combust, flare, flame, inferno, blaze, barrage, fervour, passion, excitement, accelerant, arsonist, backdraft, sparkle, flash, zeal, enthusiasm, zest, match, ignite, kindle, burn, torch, cremate, set fire, shell, arouse, spur, animate, flammable, alight, blinding, brisk, coal, expansive, explosive, hazardous, hellish, infernal, pyrotechnic, warm, smokeless, sulphur, white-hot, blistering, boiling, searing, sizzling, dynamic, lust, ember, fireball, blacken, crackle, consume, flicker, glow, hiss, incinerate, pop, rage, roast, scintillate, scorch, spread, cinder, chimney, pyre, smoke, sorcerer, soot, thermal, volcanic, coerce, impel, urge, explode, induce, gamble, creative, sharp, sting, prick, prickle, rash, energy, transformation, sexuality,

Earth-Element Words

Grounded, rooted, disciplined, rules, boundaries, restriction, results, routine, reliable, responsible, practical, leader, organised, solid, loyal, thoughtful, deliberation, decisive, safe, stable, mud, brick, loam, pottery, dust, dirt, filth, sand, soil, burrow, den, hole, cave, sanctuary, retreat, still, silent, land, gravity, death, rebirth, wisdom, nature, plants, animals, money, abundance, currency, prosperity, riches, wealth, sturdiness, stubborn, determined, time, structure, stability, tradition, age, ambition, career, work.

This is an opportunity for you to add more earth-based words:

Air-Element Words

Lightness, communication, mind, intellect, creative, unpredictable, conversation, wind, breeze, draughty, sky, ventilation, gust, harmony, aerate, freshen, refresh, fan, purify, oxygenate, to hand out, proclaim, speak, divulge, stifle, conceal, censor, transmit, broadcast, curious, independent, talkative, intellectual, connector, networker, nonconformist, genius, rebellious, hurricane, tornado, storm, cyclone, flighty, fly, freedom, travel, debate, language, learning.

Add more air-element words here:

Water-Element Words

Feelings, imagination, care, tenderness, vulnerable, secretive, private, addiction, empathic, compassionate, nursing, intuitive, psychic, rain, lake, sea, ocean, creek, river, stream, beck, ford, puddle, bay, rapids, coastline, shoreline, current, waves, lagoon, pool, splash, drip, drop, irrigate, wet, wash, bathe, dampen, moist, douse, soak, sprinkle, flood, down, lather, soak, sponge, corrode, waterlog, watermark.

Add more water-element words here:

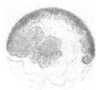

Spirit-Element Words

Silence, stillness, emptiness, existential, resonance, unrestrained, omniscient, omnipresence.

Add more spirit-element words here:

Your Elemental Narrative

As the writer of stories, has it occurred to you that you will have a writing style that reflects one of the elements?

Ideally, as we develop our writing voice we will become multi-elemental in our narrative, however, it is helpful to know which style we gravitate to and where our strength is so that we can make the most of it, and also learn to develop the others.

Fire
If your narrative is lit up with plenty of drama and action, you're a fire-dominant writer. Your stories feature a hero on a journey. It's possible that the stories involve elements of danger, destruction and rescue.

Earth
If you build your writing on the foundation of creating believable settings, your style is earth. The reader or listener will feel as if they are there in the world you've created. Your writing actively engages the senses.

Air

If you write from the element of air your narrative will be defined by the uncovering of answers. Your work is intimately involved in posing questions, then leaving clues. It has a mysterious feel to it.

Water

If you're a writer who splashes about in the water element, your writing is character based, and you delve into what the person needs, is looking for, and the changes involved in their journey.

Spirit

Can you see what I see? Can you hear what I hear? Can you feel what I feel? Can you taste what I taste? Can you sense what I sense? If you're a fifth-element writer, there'll be a sense of omniscient view in how you narrate.

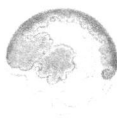

The Elements & Personality

Back in the 5th Century BCE, the Greek philosophers talked of four elements as the basis for life. It was Aristotle who included the heavenly element of Spirit (ether). The Greek astrologers assigned four human temperaments to reflect the four elements.

The four temperaments can help us to understand ourselves and others, and is a focal point in personal development. Each of us has a primary temperament, and it is accompanied by a secondary one. This is our nature, not something we've developed.

The Four Temperaments are:
- Choleric (*Fire*)
- Melancholic (*Earth*)
- Sanguine (*Air*)
- Phlegmatic (*Water*)

Choleric is considered to have tendencies like being irritable, feisty and quick-tempered. This temperament is enthusiastic, strong willed, ambitious, filled with energy and confidence. Where they can improve themselves is by developing empathy.

Melancholic types are considered solid, reliable, quiet, analytical. Passionate, well organised and loyal. This temperament has strong ideals and likes to connect with people at a deep level. A tendency to depression or perfectionism needs to be overcome in their quest for personal development.

Sanguine is optimistic; they're the sociable, people lovers. Everyone likes them, and they're happiest in and around other people. The area for self-development lies around avoiding anything difficult, whether in relationships or taking on too much.

Phlegmatic is considered peaceful and relaxed. This temperament is found in the person who has deep-level listening skills, naturally empathic, and comfortable with the simple pleasures in life. Their superpower is being calm in chaos. The area of personal growth is learning to initiate projects and asserting themselves in areas of conflict.

Extroverts
Choleric and Sanguine (fire and air)

Introverts
Melancholic and Phelgmatic (earth and water)

Task Focused
Choleric and Melancholic (fire and earth)

People Focused
Sanguine and Phlegmatic (air and water)

Temperament Orientation
Fire: Choleric → Results
Earth: Melancholic → Quality
Air: Sanguine → People
Water: Phlegmatic → Service

Elemental Journey

As a celebrant, we weave our way through this world with word medicine and are rooted in ritual. In essence, we are healers. Our own healing is paramount.

Explore your memories of relationship to each element. It might be from childhood or to do with current experiences.

Consider your senses, and how you've experienced these elements in ways that might seem positive and those that are not so pleasant.

Ways of Living with the Fire Element

☼ Watch the sunrise or sunset as a daily practice
☼ Cooking and baking
☼ Light your fire
☼ Lanterns
☼ Lamps
☼ Vase of sunflowers
☼ Create a noontide ritual
☼ Be brave and feel the fear
☼ Have a bonfire or firepit
☼ Sauna
☼ Candlelight
☼ Wear fire colours: red, orange, yellow
☼ Use oranges, chillis, cloves and cinnamon
☼ Coffee
☼ Running or aerobic exercise
☼ Sunshine
☼ Compete
☼ Create

Fire Journal:
How has the fire element burned away anything I didn't need?

When has fire ignited my passions and purpose?

What do I need to create to bring vitality, creativity and passion to me?

Is there anything in my life I can burn off?

What is the best way for me to enliven my body through movement?

In what ways do I include this element in my life?

Ways of Living with the Earth Element

♣ Barefoot on grass, sand or soil
♣ Collect sand from the beach
♣ A bowl of salt for protection, by the front door
♣ Lucky coins or a pentacle
♣ Branches & leaves
♣ Grow flowers, fruits, vegetables and herbs
♣ Keep houseplants
♣ Collect pottery
♣ Learn to make pottery
♣ Eat seasonal foods
♣ Forest bathing
♣ Engage your senses
♣ Curate a collection of crystals
♣ Keep pebbles and stones in your home
♣ Step outside in the evenings to appreciate the night
♣ Practise eco-friendly living, such as recycling and reusing
♣ Grow fresh flowers
♣ Keep a gratitude journal

Earth Journal:
When did earth ground me?

How has earth healed me?

Has earth eroded my abrasive edges?

In what ways do I include the earth element in my life?

Where do I have solid boundaries?

What structures, routines or rituals anchor me?

Ways of Living with the Air Element

◊ Fly a kite
◊ Feel the wind on your face
◊ Sleep with the window open
◊ Wear white, silver, yellow or blue
◊ Hang bells or chimes in your home or garden
◊ Ring a bell in each room of your home to shift the energy
◊ Learn how to use a singing bowl
◊ Write letters and cards
◊ Collect feathers or fans
◊ Light incense
◊ Debating
◊ Networking
◊ Night classes
◊ Phone calls

◊ Enjoy an electrical storm
Air Journal:
In what ways has this element helped me speak with honesty?

When have I placed a Cosmic Order and directed my desires?

How can I bring more of this element into my life?

What is my communication style?

Do I listen carefully? That is, do I let the other person finish their sentence without butting in to share a relatable story?

Ways of Living with the Water Element

≈ Gather items from alongside streams, lakes, rivers
≈ Beachcombing
≈ Bowl of sand
≈ Seaglass
≈ Chalice of water
≈ Seashells
≈ Driftwood
≈ Coral
≈ Willow
≈ Seaweed
≈ Fern
≈ Infuse water under the full Moon
≈ Swim
≈ Swim with dolphins
≈ Walk in the rain
≈ Long hot bath or shower
≈ Jacuzzi or hot tub
≈ Drink herb teas
≈ Eat leafy green salads
≈ Listen to the rain on a tin roof
≈ Drink water

Water Journal:

When has this element washed away my wounds?

How have I soothed heartache?

Do I allow myself to cry?

When was the last time I followed my feelings?

Is it natural for me to be compassionate and empathic?

Do I listen to my intuition?

How can I bring more of this element into my life?

Ways of Living with the Spirit Element

∞ Create circles
∞ Use infinity symbols
∞ Sleep with an amethyst geode by your bed
∞ Drink lotus tea
∞ Anoint with blue lotus oil
∞ Wear black, white, purple, silver
∞ Commune with angels
∞ Meditate
∞ Prayer
∞ Offer blessings
∞ Fast from food or speaking
∞ Practise living with silence

Spirit Journal:
Have I allowed Spirit to bring stillness to my soul?

Do I allow silence to settle into me?

Can I write down my dreams as a way of listening to Spirit?

Is there a way I can make a meditative mandala to focus on Spirit?

Am I living the life I want?

Am I free?

Am I living with purpose?

Am I consciously connected with my highest self?

In what ways can I develop more awareness of Spirit?

"What if our religion was each other.
If our practice was our life.
If prayer, our words.
What if the temple was the Earth.
If forests were our church.
If holy water - the rivers, lakes, and ocean.
What if meditation was our relationships.
If the teacher was life.
If wisdom was self-knowledge.
If love was the centre of our being."
- Ganga White

Calling in the Six Directions

Although it is common for a celebrant officiating a pagan ceremony to Call in the Four Directions, my practice calls in six: North, East, South, West, Above & Below.

These correlate to the five elements:
Fire (South)
Earth (North)
Air (East)
Water (West)
Spirit (Above & Below)

How will you call?

You'll find a way that you have a natural affinity with when working with the directions and elemental correspondences. Some people work with a medicine wheel, Celtic, or other indigenous way. Many people start with the East: sunrise and new beginnings. This makes sense, and if this is your way there's no reason to change it. Some people call them in order of the zodiac: fire, earth, air, water (South, North, East, West).

My way, these days, is to anchor us with the North (midnight), for solidity, strength and grounding, and to call the directions in *deosil* (way of the Sun), and to close the directions *widdershins* (contrary to the way of the Sun).

An example from one of my ceremonies:

The Six Directions
We stand beneath the skies above.
We come in peace, and call the spirit of this land:
Be with us now.

Whatever needs to be here, be here.
Whatever needs to leave, leave.

(Call in deosil; Sunwise)

With this crystal of Mother Earth, we dream forth the Keeper of the North.
(place amethyst on the altar on a piece of moss)
We call to you guardian of the fertile soils,
darkness of night,
stones of our ancestors and ancestresses,
and the silence of the wild owl.

We ask that you bless Lucy and Ruben with courage when the darkness of life falls upon them. Give them endurance. Bestow upon them the strength of resilience and commitment to this marriage. Lucy and Ruben, may you always have a stable homestead to return to at the end of each day.

~

With this bell, we invoke the Keeper of the East.
(turn to the east, ring bell, and place on altar)
This is the path of awakening. The light of the rising sun. The gift of the new day.

We invite the song of the blackbird
Whoosh of the eagle's wing
And welcoming winds.

Keeper of the East, you are the breath upon which we speak. May this couple communicate with ease and grace, and grow in shared silences.

~

With the light of this candle, we invoke the Keeper of the South.
(candle in lantern)
This is the way of courage, vitality and passion.

And so we ask that the spirits of the sacred flame bless this day with light. Keeper of the South, send warmth to comfort this couple when they're cold and weary. May your fires bring brightness to all of their days.

~

With this libation to Mother Earth, a gift of spring water infused under the Moon, we call to the Keeper of the West.
(pour water on the earth)
We call to you and beckon the flow of the changing tides. This is the way of tender feelings.

We face the West, the direction of sundown. One day, our own Sun will go down over the horizon. When that time comes, may this couple bring with them the brilliant and beautiful colours of the love they shared. May you be nourished by the cleansing of raindrops, be strengthened by the deep lakes, and fullness of the sea.

(Raise hands to the sky)
We welcome the spirits of all that is Above:
Silent Stars, Shining Sun, Silvery Moon:
the conscious and unconscious Cosmos.
(Touch the earth below)

We welcome the love of Mother Earth, and all she holds dear: creatures and crystals, soil and stones, flowers and fragrances. We give thanks for you, and to you, with deep appreciation.

As above, so below.

(To everyone present) Could you each place your hand over your heart?
(hands over hearts, and wait a moment…)

Take a few moments to remember your sacred breath: the giver of life. We give thanks for the ancient heartbeat that connects us to all living beings, to our ancestors and ancestresses, and to the One Heart. Beings of love and light are called in here today. Our circle is safe.

At the end of the ceremony:
As we close this circle, let us give thanks to those we love, near and far, seen and unseen.
(Widdershins – Against the way of the Sun)

Keeper of the West, thank you for sharing the feelings of this day.
Linger if you like.
Depart if you dare.
Blessed Be.

Keeper of the South, thank you for the passion in this marriage.
Linger if you like.
Depart if you dare.
Blessed Be.

Keeper of the East, thank for your whispers that show this couple the art of communication.
Linger if you like.
Depart if you dare.
Blessed Be.

Keeper of the North, we thank you for being the foundation of their life together.
Linger if you like.
Depart if you dare.
Blessed Be.

All that is above, and all that is below. We thank you.

May this circle be released but unbroken. May the remaining energy in this circle dance with your dreams across the whole of your lives.

Elemental Blessing

Spirit, be with me now.
Keeper of the North, honour me with your silence that I may know myself in your stillness.

Keeper of the East, show me the path of truth-telling so that my words and intentions come from a place of honesty.

Keeper of the South, ignite my heart, and infuse my days with passion so that I may live with enthusiasm.

Keeper of the West, show me how to live life fully between the bookends of my birth and my death, so that when I cross the horizon my sunset shall be one of beauty.

All That Is, may I live with gratitude and kindness. May I dwell in your Presence.

Celebrant Note: I have also spoken this collectively: "Honour us with your silence that we may know your stillness", etc.

Elemental Meditation

We are as much a part of the five elements as they are part of us. Consciously connecting with them through mantra, mandalas and meditation allows the energies to become elevated within, and is deeply healing. Your vibrational frequency shifts and you find alignment between mind, body and soul.

Mantra

I am fire
I am earth
I am air
I am water
I am spirit.

Mandala

In many spiritual traditions, a mandala is used to create sacred space and to focus one's attention. Within a circle, it is a geometric composition of symbols. Download a free mandala from one of the many craft sites, and colour it in using colours from the five elements. Alternatively, make an outdoor mandala using items from nature.

Meditation

This simple meditation can be prerecorded or you can ask a loved one to guide you through it. Maybe you'll read through it a few times first, and then guide yourself.

Create an Elemental Altar

Create an elemental altar by using one thing for each element, such as:

- *Candle for fire*
- *Crystal/moss for earth*
- *Feather for air*
- *Bowl of water*
- *Spiral or circle*

Begin by getting comfortable in a chair. Invite stillness to enter your being.

Slow your breathing down. Nice long in and out breaths. Become aware of each element. Focus on only one at a time. Now, come back to fire. Allow your breathing to remain slow and pleasantly rhythmic. Let the flame remind you of the fire within you.

Are you expressing your passion? Do you feel lit up in your day-to-day life? What can fire teach you?

Be mindful of your breathing. Now, bring your focus to the earth element. Are you rooted in your life? Do you have a sense of stability no matter what is going on in the world? How deep are your roots? Where are you planted?

Again, be mindful of your breathing. Let the air element come to mind. Where do you draw your inspiration? Have you let your dreams soar on the breeze?

Once again, be mindful of your breathing. Reflecting on the element of water now:
Are you going with the flow? Are you nourishing your emotional nature?

Come back to your breathing. Now it is time to allow your awareness to settle on your understanding of the element of spirit.
Breathe. Be Still. Know that you are one with All That Is.

Feel yourself held within the sacred space of that energy. In your own time, come back to the present moment. Alternatively, you can free your mind from any questions and simply allow the energy of the elements to speak for themselves.

"With life as short as a half taken breath,
don't plant anything but love."
— Rumi

About the Author

Veronika Sophia Robinson is an intuitive, empathic Heart-led Celebrant in the north of England who has been officiating ceremonies since 1995. Along with her husband, Paul, she's the co-founder and co-tutor at Heart-led Ceremonies Celebrant Training. Veronika mentors celebrants from around the world and leads celebrant workshops in person and online. Veronika is an accredited Infant Loss Professional; and certified in Self-Harm and Suicide Prevention.

Amongst the many books she's authored (fiction and non-fiction), Veronika's publications include those in the Celebrant Collection: Write That Eulogy; The Successful Celebrant; Funerals for Children; The Discrimination-Free Celebrant; The Blessingway, Funeral Celebrant Ceremony Planner; and Wedding Celebrant Ceremony Planner.

For thirteen years, she enjoyed an international psychological astrology practice.

When she's not writing or working as a celebrant and celebrant trainer, Veronika can be found reading, walking in the woods or across fields, listening to classical music, enjoying plant-based cooking, soaking up sunshine, seeking adventures here and there, or walking barefoot in the garden.

www.veronikarobinson.com

About the Artist

Sarah Louise Esau is first and foremost a mother to two home-educated teens. She's married to Sean, who she met in Coogee Bay in Australia, whilst they were both traveling many years ago.

Sarah has over 20 years experience of working with young people both in mainstream and alternative settings. She's a passionate advocate for consent-based, self-directed education and has published many articles about education, the more recent ones you can find on her blog:
www.unschoolsketchbook.com

Sarah loves to be outdoors walking with her dog, Legend, and observing the changing seasons. She's been a volunteer for mcsuk since 2016, and likes to import the wonder she experiences when immersed in nature into her drawings.

Sarah has always loved to draw and finds a deep sense of peace when sketching at home with a backdrop of music playing and a cat purring nearby. You can view her illustrations on Instagram: @slesau_art

Starflower press
CELEBRANT COLLECTION

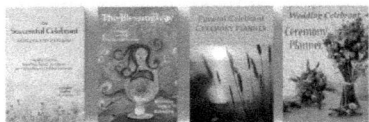

My Notes

www.ingramcontent.com/pod-product-compliance
Lightning Source LLC
Chambersburg PA
CBHW031433270326
41930CB00007B/681